Better Homes and Gardens®

W9-AZO-528

SHEDS & GAZEBOS

IDEAS AND PLANS
FOR GARDEN STRUCTURES

Meredith® Books
Des Moines, Iowa

Better Homes and Gardens Sheds and Gazebos
Writer and Principal Photographer: Dan Weeks
Editor: Larry Erickson
Photo Researcher: Harijs Priekulis
Copy Chief: Terri Fredrickson
Publishing Operations Manager: Karen Schirm
Edit and Design Production Coordinator:
  Mary Lee Gavin
Editorial and Design Assistants: Renee E. McAtee,
  Kairee Windsor
Marketing Product Managers: Aparna Pande,
  Isaac Petersen, Gina Rickert, Stephen Rogers,
  Brent Wiersma, Tyler Woods
Book Production Managers: Pam Kvitne,
  Marjorie J. Schenkelberg, Rick von Holdt,
  Mark Weaver
Contributing Designer: Tim Abramowitz
Contributing Copy Editor: Ro Sila
Contributing Proofreaders: Jane Carlson, Heidi Johnson,
  Brenda Scott Royce
Indexer: Donald Glassman

**Additional Editorial Contributions from
  Art Rep Services**
Director: Chip Nadeau
Designer: lk Design
Illustrator: Dave Brandon

Meredith® Books
Executive Director, Editorial: Gregory H. Kayko
Executive Director, Design: Matt Strelecki
Executive Editor/Group Manager: Larry Erickson
Senior Associate Design Director: Tom Wegner

Publisher and Editor in Chief: James D. Blume
Editorial Director: Linda Raglan Cunningham
Executive Director, Marketing: Jeffrey B. Myers
Executive Director, New Business Development:
  Todd M. Davis
Executive Director, Sales: Ken Zagor
Director, Operations: George A. Susral
Director, Production: Douglas M. Johnston
Business Director: Jim Leonard

Vice President and General Manager: Douglas J. Guendel

Meredith Publishing Group
President: Jack Griffin
Senior Vice President: Bob Mate

Meredith Corporation
Chairman and Chief Executive Officer: William T. Kerr
President and Chief Operating Officer: Stephen M. Lacy

In Memoriam: E. T. Meredith III (1933-2003)

Photographers
(Photographers credited may retain copyright ©
  to the listed photographs.)
L = Left, R = Right, C = Center, B = Bottom,
  T = Top

Gardensheds Web: 18-19, 28-29, 30, 31T, 31B

Gardener's Supply Company: 110, 115, 117C, 132, 133

Jamaica Cottage Shop: 8, 9, 70BR, 74, 124

Summerwood, Inc.: 11TR, 83, 86T, 86B, 170

Walpole Woodworkers: 42-43, 131B

All of us at Meredith® Books are dedicated to
providing you with the information and ideas you
need to enhance your home and garden. We welcome
your comments and suggestions. Write to us at:
Meredith Books
Home Improvement Books Department
1716 Locust St.
Des Moines, IA 50309–3023

If you would like to purchase any of our home
improvement, gardening, cooking, crafts, or home
decorating and design books, check wherever quality
books are sold. Or visit us at: bhgbooks.com

Note to the Readers: Due to differing conditions,
tools, and individual skills, Meredith Corporation
assumes no responsibility for any damages, injuries
suffered, or losses incurred as a result of following the
information published in this book. Before beginning
any project, review the instructions carefully, and if
any doubts or questions remain, consult local experts
or authorities. Because codes and regulations vary
greatly, you always should check with authorities to
ensure that your project complies with all applicable
local codes and regulations. Always read and observe
all of the safety precautions provided by
manufacturers of any tools, equipment, or supplies,
and follow all accepted safety procedures.

TABLE OF CONTENTS

CHAPTER 1
FIND YOUR INSPIRATION 4

Woodsheds 6

Ideas to Go: Roofing Research 10

Toolsheds 12

Ideas to Go: Siding Selections 16

Storage Sheds 18

　　Making an Estatement 20

　　Accessible Rusticity 22

Ideas to Go: Location, Location... . . 24

Garden Sheds 28

　　Light? Fantastic! 30

　　Taking Panes 32

　　Architectural Accents 34

　　New England Inspiration 36

　　Thinking of View 37

　　Postcard Cottage 38

　　Quick and Paintless 39

Ideas to Go: Foundations 40

Special-Purpose Sheds 42

　　Hobby Haven 44

　　Pool Shed 46

　　Rustic Retreat 48

　　Screen Room 50

Ideas to Go: Paths and Walkways ... 52

Gazebos 54

　　Instant Interest 56

　　Upslope, Downslope 58

　　Perch, Don't Plunge 60

　　Deck the Deck 62

　　Garden Grace 64

　　Camped in a Clearing 65

　　Luxurious Lighting 66

Ideas to Go: Details, Details, Details . 68

CHAPTER 2
SHED AND GAZEBO PROJECTS ... 72

Building a Woodshed 74

Building a Garden Shed 82

Building a Gazebo 98

Building a Potting Shed 110

CHAPTER 3
BUILDING BASICS 116

Site Selection and Preparation ... 118

Choosing a Building 128

Choosing a Style 130

Choosing a Plan 132

Choosing a Source 134

Choosing a Product Type 135

Choosing Materials 138

Finishes 150

Tools 152

Resources 168

Buying Guide 170

Glossary 171

Index 174

Metric Conversions 176

FIND YOUR INSPIRATION

Need a little extra storage space? Are you longing for a potting shed that can also serve as a private retreat? Perhaps you'd like a place to sit in shaded comfort and enjoy your landscape, or a place to stash next winter's firewood. The following pages are chock-full of beautiful sheds and gazebos—and great ideas about how to site, embellish, landscape, and use them. You'll also find tips, hints, and techniques to help you choose and build your own structures.

Most buildings featured are available as plans, lumber packages, or kits from several manufacturers. When you see a building you like on these pages, turn to the Buying Guide on page 170 for more information about that building. For a list of manufacturers, kit suppliers, and plan publishers, turn to the resource list on page 168. Many of these companies have websites and toll-free numbers for additional information.

But first, turn the page for an inspiring, idea-filled tour of distinctive and useful outbuildings.

Woodsheds

If you use your wood-burning fireplace or stove more than just occasionally, a woodshed is a great asset. These structures help your wood season quickly so it's ready to burn when you need it. They also protect wood from dampness and rot once it has seasoned, prolonging storage time. Woodsheds contain the woodpile, making the fuel easier to stack and retrieve. Finally, they shed snow, so you don't have to dig your firewood out after a blizzard.

Nor are woodsheds all utility: They have a handsome, even romantic, quality about them. The neatly stacked wood adds a rustic backdrop to a yard or garden. Split wood, especially, gives off a pleasant aroma, perfuming your yard while it seasons. And the structure and its contents are a year-round reminder of cozy cool-weather fires.

Woodsheds are available in many forms—as plans, as ready-to-assemble kits, and as lumber packages. Their simplicity puts woodsheds among the easiest outbuilding projects to build—a great way to test and practice your carpentry skills before you tackle a larger, more complex shed.

▶ **This woodshed has a gabled roof that sheds snow equally to the front and back, preventing a large snowpile on just one side. Built on skids, the shed rests on concrete blocks that have been leveled to correct for a sloping site. A gravel pad beneath the shed allows good drainage, so frost heaves won't throw the building out of shape. The gravel extends beyond the roof's drip line, providing a place for runoff to drain and minimizing mud. Painted to match the home it serves, the building has a green metal roof that blends with the surrounding foliage. The shed faces south, so solar exposure and prevailing winds help speed the wood's drying.**

▶ Easy does it: Look for opportunities to take advantage of existing walls. This little lean-to structure does the work of a woodshed, without putting you to much work building it.

Size your woodshed according to your available yard space and the amount of wood you need to store. If you buy seasoned wood, you'll need only as much storage as the amount you actually burn. If you season your own wood, consider a two-sided shed that'll hold enough wood for two years. Such a shed is open on two sides, with a partition running down the middle. One side is for dry wood that's ready to burn this season. The other side is for green wood that will be ready to burn next season. Each year, you alternate usage of each side.

◀ Measuring 10 feet long by 4 feet deep, this wood bin has a saltbox roof design. The rearward slope directs most of the rain and snow to the ground behind the shed. Situated at the edge of its lot, this shed backs up to the woods so the owner doesn't have to transport heavy rounds of unsplit wood across the yard.

SITING A WOODSHED

At least two schools of thought exist regarding the best location for a woodshed:

Place it close to the house to make firewood retrieval less of a chore in cold, wet weather. This option works best if you buy seasoned, bug-free wood that won't mess up your dooryard with sawdust and splinters and endanger your house's structure by exposing it to wood-boring insects that may lurk in the firewood.

Place it in a remote location. People who cut, split, and season their own wood often prefer to confine the noisy, messy, buggy operation of firewood processing to a back corner of the yard. A remote location may also allow you to more easily orient the shed so it's exposed to ample sunshine and a prevailing breeze, both of which will help season your wood more quickly, reducing the "wait time" between harvesting and burning. If you choose the more remote location, create a path that's wide, smooth, and firm enough to allow you to back your truck or trailer up to the shed for unloading wood. The same path can serve as a route over which to carry seasoned firewood to the house in a garden cart or with a lawn tractor and trailer. A covered wood bin on the porch or deck can store those cartloads of wood right outside the door so you can bring them into the house as you burn them, a few pieces at a time.

That way, you always have access to both piles—the seasoned wood to burn and the green wood you'll add to the stack as you cut and split logs.

Because green wood gives off moisture, woodsheds are best built from rot-resistant species or pressure-treated lumber. Many owners choose to leave their sheds in their natural state so that they'll blend in with the wood stacked inside them. Others choose to paint sheds to match or contrast with their homes or other nearby outbuildings.

Wood Storage Alternatives

If your wood consumption is modest and you're already planning a garden, storage, tool, or potting shed, you could dedicate a space—perhaps along an interior wall—to storing wood. Do that only if the wood is already dried and bug-free, as the humidity and insects introduced by wet or buggy wood can damage the building and its contents.

Alternatively, consider adding a lean-to section on the back or side of an outbuilding to accommodate your firewood. Most outbuilding manufacturers offer custom design services, and it's often a simple matter to extend a building's roofline to accommodate a covered storage space. Leave the outward-facing wall of the lean-to open, both to allow the wood to continue drying, and to make retrieving it easier. It's difficult, if not impossible, to open and close doors with an armload of firewood.

◀ Here, a main wood storage section holds about a cord of split wood. One end is partitioned off and makes a handy place to store kindling, splitting mauls, and yard tools. This same basic design can be built with a lockable door on the toolshed section for increased security.

ROOFING RESEARCH

One of the joys of building a shed or gazebo is the chance to use character-enhancing materials that might be inappropriate—or too expensive—to use on a residence. That's especially true when it comes to roofing materials. These small buildings often have roofs that are low enough to readily be seen—both from the ground and from the upper stories of your house. Some sheds have quite steeply pitched roofs, adding to that surface's visibility. And gazebos often sport elaborate roof designs that look their best when surfaced with a premium material. Here are some materials that expand your choices beyond the generic three-tab asphalt roof shingle:

CEDAR SHINGLES

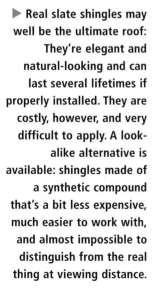

◀ Sawn from clear, knot-free cedar, shingles are a traditional and long-lasting choice for shed and gazebo roofs. A shingle roof gains character as it ages: The shingles typically warp, shrink, and swell slightly, creating a more organic look; often lichen or moss will grow on them as well, making the building seem a part of the natural landscape.

▶ Real slate shingles may well be the ultimate roof: They're elegant and natural-looking and can last several lifetimes if properly installed. They are costly, however, and very difficult to apply. A look-alike alternative is available: shingles made of a synthetic compound that's a bit less expensive, much easier to work with, and almost impossible to distinguish from the real thing at viewing distance.

FAUX SLATE

CEDAR SHAKES

▲ These thin, random-width pieces of cedar resemble shingles, but are split by hand rather than sawn to thickness. They have a rough, grainy, irregular texture that gives lots of depth and character to a surface, even when the shakes are new. Shingles and shakes are relatively expensive and although they're not terribly difficult to work with, are more time-consuming to apply than manufactured roofing materials.

METAL

▲ Moderate cost, great durability, and a wide selection of colors make metal roofs another excellent choice. The material comes in panels, cuts easily with a circular saw fitted with a metal-cutting blade, and fastens with rubber-grommeted nails for a waterproof installation.

CAPPING IT ALL OFF

Like a finial on a piece of fine furniture, nothing caps off a building like a little roof adornment. You'll find three popular ways to go: cupola, weather vane, and lightning rod. All three have a long tradition of use on outbuildings, and all can serve important functions in addition to their decorative ones.

▲ Cupolas were once an essential part of an old barn's ventilation system: Hot air would rise to the top of the building, where the chimney-like cupola would let it escape through louvered vents on all four sides. Purely decorative cupolas, such as the one above, often simply adorn a shed's ridge. Conversely, gazebos often have functional cupolas such as the one at left.

▶ Weather vanes also traditionally capped vintage barns; they're informative in addition to adding a dash of ornament. Rarely seen on gazebos, weather vanes show up frequently on sheds, either atop a cupola or mounted directly to the roof. Unlike cupolas, which are always centered, weather vanes can be mounted in the center of the ridge or at either end.

▲ Lightning rods were insurance against fire, especially to barns on exposed hilltops. Though they served the very practical purpose of grounding atmospheric electrical charges, they were often things of beauty as well, wrought from highly conductive copper and often incorporating a colored-glass or ceramic ball into the design. The reproduction above recreates the charm of high-style Victorian rods. As with weather vanes, lightning rods can be mounted in the center or at either end of the ridgepole.

TOOLSHEDS

The enemies of tools are "wear and where." A toolshed can save your tools from wear, protecting them damage. And it can save you from the aggravation of wondering around the yard grumbling "now where did I leave those pruning shears?"–hoping you won't find them rusting under the hedge.

For many, the backyard is an outdoor "room," a defined space with a character and a purpose. A toolshed is its closet, a storage spot that can be as simple as a box or as novel as a dream.

Even if all you need is a place to store your long-handled yard tools, you don't have to settle

▶ **It's all here: storage shelves, tool hangers, floor space for the big stuff, windows to usher in plenty of light, plus even a window box to uphold a bit of nature. Sheds embrace the stuff of life.**

▶ **"Two faced" can be a good thing. This clever shed stores tools on its yard side, outdoor furniture on its deck side.**

for an injection-molded plastic bin from the discount store. For not much more trouble or money, you can knock together a charming little shed that'll not only keep your tools dry but also add some structure and whimsy to your yard.

For a small shed, you can mimic the proportions and texture of a classic outhouse. These little buildings are small enough to plunk down just about anywhere. Want to keep your gardening tools right in the garden in summer and your snow shovel beside the drive in the winter? Just pick the building up with a cart and change locations (and contents) as needed.

These buildings have the most charm if they're constructed of recycled materials, as are the ones shown below, but you can achieve a similar effect with rough-sawn lumber (available from sawmills) and hand-split cedar shakes.

▶ Simple wooden pegs offer simply wonderful solutions to the problem of where to keep yard tools. Home centers abound with commercial variations. All serve the same goal: keeping tools readily at hand rather than clumsily under foot.

◀ A pair of country classics: Fashioned from recycled lumber, these sheds hold nostalgia as well as tools. The one at far left spans a stone pathway. Tools line up along one side; a small potting bench fills the opposite wall. The other shed sports a jaunty roof of recycled corrugated metal.

Contemporary classic

This shed proves you don't have to use recycled lumber to get a vintage look. Constructed of materials found on classic rural American buildings, it has an aesthetic that's upscale rustic. Corrugated, galvanized sheet steel walls, lattice doors, and a cedar shake roof contribute lots of texture and character. And because the materials are quite durable, the shed shouldn't require much maintenance.

Perched on the edge of a brick patio in a small urban lot, this little building replaced a yew hedge. Like the hedge, it blocks a view of a neighbor's garage and lends a sense of enclosure to the small patio. To ease the budget, it was set

▲ Corrugated metal weaves a textural element into this shed's facade. Situated next to a patio, the shed stores yard and garden tools and supplies while effectively blocking a less-than-ideal view of a neighbor's garage.

on a pea-gravel foundation rather than one of poured concrete.

To make the most of both the shed's interior and the patio, the building was fitted with sliding doors on the side facing the patio. Hinged lattice panels to the left of the structure block unattractive views and swing open for access to the area behind the shed. An additional swing-open door on the shed's gable end leads to a separate trash compartment and allows the cans to roll easily out to the curb.

▶ A separate compartment on the gable end of this shed houses trash containers and has its own access door. The trellis supports a porcelain berry vine.

▼ Lattice doors allow airflow for ventilation. Screening stapled on the interior of the doors prevents birds and small animals from nesting in the shed.

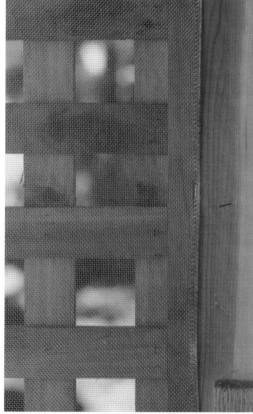

▶ Gable peak detailing adds visual interest. The ridge cap finial complements the metal siding.

SIDING SELECTIONS

As with roofing, so with siding: Due to these buildings' diminutive sizes, you can afford to cover them with materials too pricey or too rustic to use in cladding most houses.

If you like a building but would prefer a different kind of siding from what is offered, ask for alternatives. Some building manufacturers offer only one type of siding per building; others provide a range of options.

Here–from the fail-safe to the funky–are some you might consider:

ROUGH-SAWN BOARD

▲ This is perhaps the simplest siding there is: boards butted up to one another and nailed vertically in place over the building frame. Wind—and occasionally some moisture—can find its way through the gaps between these boards, making this an ideal siding method for woodsheds, where ventilation is a plus, but inappropriate for structures that must be completely weathertight.

RANDOM-WIDTH, ROUGH-SAWN BOARD-AND-BATTEN

▲ Simple, inexpensive, durable, and weathertight, board-and-batten siding clads millions of barns and sheds worldwide. It's the same as board siding, above, except a narrow board—a batten—is nailed over the joint between the siding boards. "Random-width" indicates that the boards used for siding are run-of-the-mill—literally, whatever width the log being sawed allowed—rather than a fixed dimension, further reducing the cost of this siding.

TIN CAN

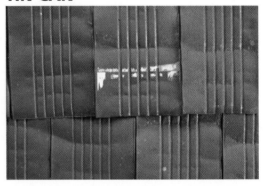

▲ During the Depression, thrifty homesteaders cut the ends off tin cans, slit the cans, and pounded them flat. Then they covered buildings with them, nailing them on in an alternating, overlapping pattern like shingles. Painted or left to rust, the material is an early example of recycling. A more colorful variant—and one that takes ingenuity and patience to accumulate— is the use of old license plates as siding. Old metal signs also can be used, overlapping them in a random, crazy-quilt pattern.

CEDAR SHINGLE

▲ Traditional, longlasting, and pricey, cedar shingles can be used for wall sheathing as well as roofing. So can their hand-split cousins, cedar shakes.

CEDAR CLAPBOARD

▲ Clear, smooth-planed, wedge-profile boards are nailed on in a horizontal, overlapping pattern that offers cedar's warmth and durability in a more formal dress than shingles or shakes. Cedar clapboard siding is generally stained or left to weather naturally. If you want to paint a clapboard building, you can save a lot of money by ordering pine clapboards instead of cedar.

LAP

▲ Lap siding overlaps like clapboard and is available in a variety of species and in various engineered-wood compositions. It generally features a rough-sawn, flat face and a machined lip that forms a lap joint with the piece of siding above and below it. It's another traditional option—less formal and more rural in flavor than clapboard but in the same family.

TONGUE AND GROOVE

▲ Generally installed vertically for increased weather resistance, tongue-and-groove siding has a refined, contemporary look. It's a great choice for a building that you'll be spending time in, such as a potting shed, as the inside is as handsome as the outside.

TEXTURED 111

▲ "Tee-one-eleven," as it's universally referred to, is a sheet plywood siding with a rough-sawn, boardlike face on one side. Inexpensive and easy to install, T-111 is available in varying qualities. The best quality has few voids and knots, both of which can lead to insect damage, rot, or both. Good-quality T-111 looks good and is reasonably durable if it's painted promptly—especially on end grain—and periodically thereafter.

STORAGE SHEDS

If your car is getting elbowed out of its garage space by the riding mower and a family of bicycles or your kids' yard toys, you need more than a toolshed to put things to rights. A walk-in storage shed with a floor of some kind (even if it's only pea gravel) and perhaps some shelves and hangers will go a long way toward alleviating the clutter.

Not too many years ago, you had a couple of choices: hire a contractor to build a shed from scratch or settle for a flimsy, noisy, stamped-steel shed that was prone to rust, hard to hang things in, and unstable under heavy snow.

Now you have numerous options, from handsome, ready-to-assemble cedar buildings that come shipped as panels and can be erected in an afternoon or weekend, to a completed structure delivered by truck directly to your site. You'll learn more about assembly and delivery options later in this book. First, take a look at the gallery of shed installations on the following pages. You'll see that storage sheds can be as attractive as they are practical and can enhance anything from a small suburban yard to a sprawling estate.

▶ This little storage shed, with its copper-topped cupola, cedar shingle roof, oversized window, flower box, and trellis, makes a charming addition to a backyard garden.

MAKING AN ESTATEMENT

A dding a storage shed can be as much an aesthetic move as a practical one. A handsome, well-placed shed can do many things in addition to sheltering equipment: It can add structure to a yard; provide a destination point for a road or path; punctuate a wall, hedge, fence, or border; provide a backdrop for a patio or outdoor seating area; serve as a support for decorative vines or climbing plants; offer a focal point for a view from the house; or enhance any style, material, or color scheme established by the house.

This shed does all of those things. The owner of the lakeside property is an amateur landscape architect who designed the many flagstone paths

■ Traditional barn styling dressed in a crisp, two-tone paint scheme creates a picturesque backdrop to a flagstone seating area. Stone walls contribute to the shed's New England flavor and provide a sense of enclosure to the "barnyard" patio.

◀ A well-sited shed looks good from many angles. This one was carefully positioned to give the eye a place to pause along the sweeping curve of the stone wall before continuing along the rock ledge to the picturesque lake beyond. The shed's blue trim echoes the color of the stream-fed lake; the blue-gray siding blends in with the granite wall and flagstone pavers.

and granite walls that grace his grounds. He incorporated a storage shed into his plans largely to add a destination and some visual interest to the yard. The shed's extra storage capacity is only a secondary benefit; two large garages and several other outbuildings were already on the property.

Nonetheless, the new shed sees lots of service, too: It stores wheelbarrows, mowers, and other yard and garden paraphernalia. It also serves as a staging location for caterers, allowing them to serve party guests enjoying the lakeside view from the patio. In winter, it provides shelter for lawn furniture and planters.

▲ Mortared rock forms the building's foundation, visually tying it to the ground and surrounding stone walls. The foundation sits a few inches inside the building's perimeter, allowing water drainage from the site and good air circulation around the bottom edge of the textured sheet siding.

▲ Situated at the end of a winding path that passes an old stone guesthouse, the new shed adds further depth to the scene while screening a neighbor's house from view.

ACCESSIBLE RUSTICITY

A basic shed design can be endlessly customized to meet different tastes and needs. Many plan services and building manufacturers can customize a building for a fee; some offer a list of modifications that can be included in a building package when you place your order.

Building makers also may offer you a choice of configurations, letting you choose from swinging, double, Dutch, or sliding doors and fixed or opening windows of various designs and placement. You might wish to add exterior embellishments such as weather vanes, cupolas, lightning rods, flower boxes or flowerpot holders, and trellises. Interior options may include a choice of flooring materials, shelving, lofts, workbenches, potting benches, or other built-in amenities.

This shed, situated at the back of a suburban yard, is similar in size and proportion to the shed pictured on pages 14 and 15. Differences in materials, finishes, options, and accessories give it a completely different look.

Vertical cedar siding coated with two coats of an exterior-grade clear wood finish enhances the rustic character developed by the hayloft door and block and tackle. Sliding doors glide open on reproductions of century-old track hardware. Finally, the shed is easily accessible to the owner, who uses a wheelchair, via a smooth paving-stone path that connects to the driveway.

▲ A hayloft and hoist, cedar siding, and lots of vintage-style black-iron hardware give this shed a rustic Western look. Cedar is naturally rot-resistant and can be left to weather to a light gray. In this case, staining and sealing the wood gives it a warm, mellow tone.

▶ Easily accessible from wheelchair height, the custom extension on the sliding door's spring-bolt latch eases entry to this shed—as do the ramp and smooth paving-stone path.

▲ The crushed-gravel pad on which this building was placed was extended to become a landscape element that sets off the building. The gravel also prevents mud from splashing up and soiling the siding during heavy rains.

LOCATION, LOCATION, LOCATION

NESTLED OUT OF SIGHT

Unlike toolsheds and even some small woodsheds, storage sheds aren't all that easy to move, so you'll want to choose your location carefully. Here are some popular options:

◀ This 8×10 cedar shed slips neatly into a small clearing in a corner of the yard; a cedar hedge and some other plantings screen it from view from both the house and the street.

■ **Pros:** Not inclined to finish, embellish, decorate, and landscape your shed? Then this is a great option. This way, too, the shed doesn't take away precious open lawn space.

■ **Tip:** Don't allow trees or other vegetation to overhang the shed too closely, as good air circulation is an excellent antidote to dampness and rot. Periodically clear the shed's roof of fallen leaves, which can trap moisture. Finally, periodically remove weak or dead branches from nearby trees so a storm won't send one crashing through your shed's roof.

SMACK AT THE END OF THE DRIVEWAY

◀ If your drive dead-ends in a tangle of woods, site your shed there.

■ **Pros:** It'll provide a definite focal point, especially if you paint it a bright barn red as this one is. Other benefits: If your drive is level, you can use it for a ready-made foundation and perhaps as a flooring surface as well. Contents—such as mowers, snowblowers, garden tractors, and wheeled trash containers— are easily wheeled out. And if you need a place to store a delivery of something large, such as a new appliance or building materials, until you're ready to use them, the shed provides an easily accessible place.

■ **Tip:** This location isn't right for every shed and drive. If your drive slopes down, ensure that runoff can be directed away from the shed (perhaps with a drain) before you build.

BESIDE THE DRIVEWAY

▶ When your drive sweeps directly into your garage, the drive-end placement is already taken. In that case, consider a position beside the driveway.

■ **Pros:** This position offers similar convenience to an end-of-driveway location—and greater flexibility of placement and landscaping. Here, the shed backs into a front corner of the lot. A handsome, cobble-curbed flagstone path sweeps through a bed of ground cover, providing an easy-rolling path for wheeled equipment.

■ **Tip:** Many folks think a storage shed belongs against the back fence, but up-front placement is often more convenient and allows you to locate your shed where everyone can enjoy it.

ON ITS OWN ISLAND OF LANDSCAPING

▶ Many backyards in new neighborhoods offer excellent views—of other back yards. Plant your shed in the middle of the view to steal the show from the neighbors' siding. Landscape extensively and colorfully around the shed to further draw the eye.

■ **Pros:** A focalpoint shed doesn't leave you feeling walled in as a stockade fence would, it doesn't impede air circulation on breezy days, and it doesn't have to be nurtured and trimmed like a tall hedge. Plus, you get the benefit of the storage space.

■ **Tip:** Don't be shy with your landscaping. If you're trying to distract from the background, the more color the better. Add a trellis and plant flowers of varying heights and blooming times for greatest effect.

LOCATION, LOCATION, LOCATION (CONTINUED)

AT THE APEX

◀ Some pie-shaped yards just seem to peter out into nothing. Punctuate the point with your shed to accent your property's shape.

■ **Pros:** An attractive shed can emphasize the symmetry of a triangular lot. Especially if the lot is fenced or outlined with a hedge, the shed gives it a logical point to terminate that offers the eye something other than a dead-end corner upon which to rest.

■ **Tip:** Clip the angle's corner with the shed's facade so it faces squarely into the yard for greatest visual effect. Set the shed out from the fence or lot line a couple feet to allow access behind the shed. That little hidden spot is a great place for a brush pile, composter, or anything else that doesn't need to be sheltered but which you'd just as soon keep out of sight.

IN LINE WITH A GATE

◀ A gate in a fence should frame a view that includes more than a blank expanse of lawn. Put your shed in the picture.

■ **Pros:** Not only does siting your shed in line with a fence make for a nice composition, it has practical benefits, too. Have you ever tried to back a utility trailer through a series of twists and turns to reach the shed where your dead garden tractor waits to be picked up for service? If so, you'll appreciate the straight shot from gate to shed that this placement offers.

■ **Tip:** Stake out your shed's potential location with story poles (see page 124 for more information) to make sure it looks good from a variety of angles, not just when seen through the gate.

HIGH SIDE OR LOW SIDE?

When building on a slope, consider the distance from the building's entry door to the ground when you orient the building and choose a plan.

Generally a storage building should have its door on the side of the building closest to the ground in order to make lifting or rolling heavy objects into the shed easier. Such door placement also minimizes the need to build a long or steep ramp—a feature that can detract from the proportions of the building's facade.

A structure designed primarily for pleasure—a potting shed or gazebo, for instance—often benefits from facing downhill, with steps leading up to the entry if necessary. The slight elevation improves the view from the building, and a few steps often add to the facade's charm.

If you can't rotate the building to accommodate the ideal door placement, see if the manufacturer or plan publisher can modify the building or plan you like best by moving the entry door to a different side.

▲ This storage shed's door is located on the side of the building nearest the ground to facilitate moving items in and out. A short ramp, yet to be built, will allow drive-in access for a garden tractor.

▶ The porch and entry door of this garden shed face downhill, offering the gardener a commanding view of her garden and yard. Lattice gives the slightly elevated porch a traditional treatment and provides a handsome, textured backdrop for plantings.

Garden Sheds

You can be an avid gardener without a garden shed. But a well-sized, well-planned, and well-located shed in the garden makes gardening tasks a whole lot more convenient. A shed also saves your garage, deck, and patio from becoming littered and soiled with the inevitable by-products of gardening.

Garden sheds often serve multiple purposes. Like a toolshed, they can store long-handled tools. Like a yard storage shed, they can provide a garage for garden tractors, mowers, and other lawn-maintenance equipment. Their situation in the garden makes them the ideal spot to store planters and potting soil, hoses and watering cans, gardening aprons, clogs, gloves, and other attire–and, of course, special gardening tools such as garden carts, rototillers, cultivators, sprayers, and more.

Most important to many gardeners, a shed can serve as a place to pot and tend to plants. Some models with lots of windows double as greenhouses, offering a place to start seedlings or grow warm-climate plants in cooler locales.

A shed in the garden adds architectural appeal to your favorite part of the yard, too. Equip your shed with a trellis, flower boxes, or flowerpot holders, and it becomes part of the cultured landscape. It can serve as a garden focal point, a backdrop, a terminus for paths and walkways–garden design possibilities abound.

Finally, a garden shed offers yet another vantage point from which to view your garden. Most such sheds feature view-framing windows or even a small porch on which you can sit and admire your plantings. But even the simplest shed offers one of gardening's great pleasures

a shady spot to turn over a big flowerpot,

have a seat in the cool, and look out on what

you and nature have wrought in your landscape.

▼ This little garden shed offers loads of charm with its bracketed, overhanging roof, cedar shingles, and white-painted trim and trellis. It's practical, too, with separate rooms and doors: storage on the left, potting on the right.

LIGHT? FANTASTIC!

This shed was born of a great idea: Combine a traditional, gable-roof shed with huge roof windows for a space that's great for starting seeds and growing delicate plants, yet has plenty of wall and storage space, too.

The skylights are constructed of ¼-inch-thick laminated glass with cedar trim. Six tilt-open windows (four on one side, one on each end) provide ample ventilation. The rear of the shed has no window, helping the building retain heat. An arbor shelters the door and provides a place for climbers to grow.

Oriented with the windowed side and roof facing south, this shed and its surroundings extend the growing season considerably. The rock-walled raised bed in front of the shed warms up earlier in the spring than a ground-level garden would. Cold frames placed against the front of the shed warm up even more

Situated on a gentle south slope, this shed blocks the intensively planted raised bed of vegetables in front of it from cold north winds—and creates a warm microclimate there by reflecting sunlight and holding heat in its masonry foundation. The result is a microorganic garden that's productive weeks longer than usual for its growing zone—and a cozy, light-filled space from which to enjoy it.

quickly and hold heat throughout chilly spring and fall nights, thanks to the thermal mass of the shed's masonry foundation.

A large, deep potting bench against the south wall is a great place to pot and start flowers, vegetables, and more. It's so light, warm, and cozy even on cool days, thanks to its southern exposure, that the bench is ideal for using for various other hobbies and projects as well. The space under the bench stores the usual detritus of gardening out of sight. The back wall stores tools and supplies.

▲ The roof slope is calculated to make the most of a southern exposure. The boards used for the siding were painted on one side before the shed was assembled, creating a colorful backdrop and highlighting the wall's structural elements. The hatch to the left of the window opens to provide additional ventilation.

◀ The back wall is used for storage. Boards fastened just above the wall's horizontal structural members create shelves useful for storing gardening supplies; foot-long dowels fastened in pairs to the uppermost board hold long-handled garden tools.

TAKING PANES

▲ A large collection of wooden-framed windows was pieced together like a puzzle to form this unique potting shed/greenhouse. The lower walls are covered with clapboard siding.

▶ Trellises help plants climb the structure; vines have been trained to run along the eaves. Acrylic panels cut to size form the angular windows in the gables. A system of levers and handles allows opening the top windows for ventilation.

Made largely of recycled windows, this potting shed has a completely different feel from the one on page 37. Surrounded by a white picket fence, this structure oozes country-cottage charm.

The windows were left homeless as the result of a large-scale house remodeling project (similar stashes can be found at architectural salvage yards). The building was designed around the windows' dimensions; some window

◀ Inside, shelves run the length of the building just beneath the windows; they can be used for potting or for holding seedlings in starting trays. The building is set on a foundation of concrete blocks. Pea gravel—comfortable to walk on and self-draining—forms the floor.

frames were trimmed slightly to fit. Then the windows were stripped, painted, reglazed or puttied where necessary, fastened to the building's frame, and caulked at the joints to make them weathertight.

The result is a low-cost, roomy potting shed that doubles as a greenhouse and has the look of an old-fashioned conservatory.

▶ A vintage glass-paned storm door serves as the building's entry. An old folding chair repainted the same color as the shed's siding stands in as patio furniture.

ARCHITECTURAL ACCENTS

This potting-shed-and-porch combination features charming architectural detailing. The porch is narrower than the building it fronts and is slightly off-center, adding interest to the facade. It's also deep enough to accommodate an antique, two-person sleigh bench to the right of the door. The outdoor sitting area gains intimacy from a roofline that peaks just below the structure's main roof.

◀ **The more complex the design, the simpler the color scheme. So says one rule, and this handsome, well-proportioned potting shed supports it. Red accents on the door, the sleigh bench upholstery, and the rooftop lightning rod provide spark. Touches of Tudor styling add richness and textural detail.**

Faux-slate roofing has a deep-relief design in keeping with the building's textural richness and with the facade's period details. The steep roof is a Tudor tradition, too. Wrought-iron flowerpot holders beneath the window carry geraniums in season; the hardware offers an alternative to flower boxes that are more in keeping with the shed's Tudor references. A bonus: The painted iron hardware won't rot out as wooden boxes eventually will.

The shed gets its English Tudor flavoring from the king post in the porch gable, key ornaments at the roof peaks, robust railings with turned spindles, and the faux-slate roof. A subdued, monochromatic color scheme lets the detailing take center stage and allows shadows, rather than jarring colors, to provide just enough contrast.

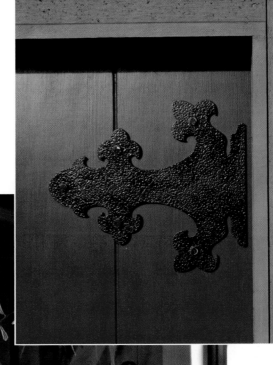

◀ Tongue-and-groove vertical siding treated with a semi-transparent stain results in rich color while allowing subtle grain variegations to show through. The false door hinges are reproductions of those found on an old church.

◀ The interior of the shed looks great, too: The tongue-and-groove siding has the same profile inside as out, creating a light, aromatic, character-filled space. To give timber-frame appeal, 4x4 posts were substituted for 2x4 studs, and diagonal braces were added at the corners. No time-consuming joinery is involved in their installation: The braces are fastened in place with wood screws and lag bolts that are countersunk and strategically placed out of view.

NEW ENGLAND INSPIRATION

▲ Inspired by traditional New England barns, this shed is dressed for the garden with trellises flanking the entry door and a window box beneath each of four symmetrically placed windows. The boxes are mounted on brackets that allow airspace between the box and sill, helping to prevent rot.

▶ Crisp white trim accents the shed's proportions and ties the structure in with the nearby white-painted garden arbor. T-111 siding provides subtle texture; its rough finish minimizes glare when the shed receives direct sunlight. The firewood-sheltering overhang matches the slope of the main roof for pleasing continuity of line.

▶ With its simple, rectangular shape, the shed complements a nearby formal garden. Often buildings are most pleasing when viewed from a slight angle so more than one side can be seen. The owner, an artist, planned the position of the shed carefully to ensure just such a perspective from the deck of her second-floor studio.

Tending a garden is so much easier when everything you need is close at hand. This handsome shed, tucked behind a low hedge between a stretch of lawn and a garden, holds the tools to maintain both. An overhang on one side shelters firewood, eliminating the need for a separate woodshed. This shed's windows are deliberately placed high on the wall, both for security (their location makes it difficult to see what's inside) and practicality, (they leave plenty of wall space beneath them for mounting shelves, hanging tools, or positioning a potting or workbench). A transom window over the door brings in additional daylight.

THINKING OF VIEW

This one-of-a-kind potting shed was inspired by the surrounding landscape. Situated on the hilltop front lawn of a Victorian farmhouse with a sweeping horizon-to-horizon vista, this structure blends with the style of the main house. Inside, plants get plenty of sunlight, and the gardener can enjoy the serenity of the countryside while potting and tending.

The owner-builder designed the building around the handsome, curved-glass windows of a county courthouse undergoing renovation. The windows were free for the asking; the rest of the period-style detailing is new—the result of decades spent studying old buildings. Stately proportions bring all the elements together.

▶ **The formal elegance of this building is right at home on the farm thanks to its immediate surroundings. Antique paving bricks, a 19th-century wrought-iron fence, and even a vintage street lamp suggest a town square in miniature for the courtly glass-sided shed.**

▲ A potting shed this substantial deserves the right landscaping to set it off. Flower beds ring the structure, a foretaste of the riot of color found inside during the growing season.

▲ Band-sawn corbels bracket the roof's handsome overhang; turned finials make the building seem to drip with ornamentation. A Victorian-inspired three-color paint treatment sets each feature off.

POSTCARD COTTAGE

Painted a crisp white and decorated to the nines, this little potting shed resembles a miniature Victorian cottage. Situated on a hillside at the end of the driveway, it's the first thing visitors see when they arrive—and invariably, the first thing they comment on.

The homeowners might have built a gazebo here, as the site commands a fine view of a nicely landscaped yard. But a see-through gazebo—especially one of naturally finished wood—would have disappeared against the forest behind it. Instead, the owners wanted a focal point.

As the view was largely in one direction (downhill, facing the house), the homeowners realized they could have most of the benefits of a gazebo and their focal point too if they chose a solid-walled garden shed with a sitting porch. To make it stand out further, the structure was painted white to contrast with the lawn and foliage. The interior's storage and potting area came as a bonus to what is primarily a favorite sitting spot and lawn ornament.

▲ A hillside location provides a picture-postcard setting complete with flower-lined flagstone path. The brown-stained lattice beneath the porch and the salvaged naturally weathered entry door complement the path's earthy hues. Solar-powered pendent lights mark the way after dusk; a final solar fixture hangs from the gable, casting a glow over the entry.

▲ An oblique view is no less pleasing; it shows off the building's metal roof and window flower box. The windows provide light and full-time ventilation; the tilt-out design prevents rain from entering the building even when the windows are open.

QUICK AND PAINTLESS

Elaborate site-built sheds are great if you have the time, money, and inclination. But sometimes what you really need is a quick, good-looking, multipurpose yard and garden shelter that doesn't cost a lot.

This combination potting and storage shed was built from a kit in less than a day. Preassembled wall and roof panels were shipped as a compact, palletized package, then fastened together by the homeowner with the help of step-by-step instructions, a power screwdriver, and a few common hand tools. Kits such as this are available in a wide variety of styles. They're standing proof that a novice can assemble a shed of premium, low-maintenance materials—a cedar shake roof, cedar lap siding, and a tongue-and-groove cedar entry door—and not have to resort to sheet steel or molded plastic.

This structure is three-quarters storage, one-quarter potting shed. The storage section—to the right rear and the left of the entry door—is windowless to make large expanses of wall available for shelving and tool hanging. The potting corner features two picture windows for daylight and views, topped with prop-open units for ventilation and more light.

► Lightweight materials and panelized construction allow this kit to be shipped economically by truck and assembled by two people in less than a day. The cedar can be stained or left to weather; either way, the material requires less work to finish and maintain than do painted structures.

▲ This shed is thoughtfully positioned at the intersection of the home's backyard play area and side yard garden. The entry door opens to the backyard, making the shed convenient for storing large yard toys. Corner windows offer views of both yards, so a potting parent can simultaneously keep an eye on the kids and enjoy garden views. A split-rail fence of matching cedar is backed with wire mesh to keep small children and pets safe inside the fenced play area and a composter is tucked behind the shed, out of view of the backyard's patio.

FOUNDATION, FOUNDATION, FOUNDATION

CONCRETE BLOCK

How you engineer the points where your shed meets the ground is key to ending up with a level, square, long-lived building. But how you treat the foundation is visually important as well. Here are some options:

◀ Simply set the building on top of of carefully positioned concrete blocks.

■ **Pros:** This foundation is best if you enjoy the way the ground around your building appears just as it is and you want the look of a building that's treading lightly on the land.

■ **Tip:** Forgo landscaping if you choose this foundation type and enjoy the natural lay of the land.

FALSE STONE FOUNDATION

◀ Build your building on concrete blocks as shown above, then build a dry-laid stone wall of rocks underneath it. The stones are real; it's called a false foundation because the rocks don't support the building's weight—the blocks behind them do.

■ **Pros:** The addition of the rocks gives your building a traditional, permanent look. Finding, moving, and placing the rocks involves considerable work but much less precision and know-how than making a real foundation of stone.

■ **Tip:** Whenever possible, use rocks from the building site rather than buying stone or importing it from elsewhere. Not only is this a much less expensive option, but the building will blend in with the landscape better.

BOXED-IN BASE

▲ Build a level pad of pea gravel or (as in this case) paving blocks and box it in with treated landscape timbers.

■ **Pros:** Landscape timbers—lag-bolted together at the corners, then spiked into the ground with lengths of steel rod—create a neat, square base that looks great in formal settings. The timbers also contain the foundation material, preventing erosion around the building.

■ **Tip:** Creating a level pad on uneven ground is much more difficult than leveling a concrete block foundation. Choose this option only if you're patient and willing to move, compact, and level a considerable amount of soil, gravel, and paving material.

▶ If you need lots of gravel to level the site, face the pad with stone on the low side(s).

■ **Pros:** The stone facing on the sloping sides of the pad has several advantages: It ties the building to the ground with a natural material, breaks up the monotony of a featureless expanse of gravel, and helps prevent erosion.

■ **Tip:** For the most pleasing appearance, choose large rocks that offer a significant contrast in scale to the gravel.

GRAVEL PAD

▲ Create a pad of gravel to level the building site. Add stone on the low side(s) to stabilize the pad and enhance its appearance.

■ **Pros:** When you have a very uneven site, you may not want the "jacked-up-in-the-air" look that you'd get with a concrete block foundation. In that case, hire a contractor to build a level gravel pad, filling the low side with gravel.

■ **Tip:** Even on a reasonably level gravel pad, use blocks for a final foundation. They're easier to level, and allow more air circulation under the shed than setting it directly on the gravel.

GRAVEL PAD WITH STONE FACING

Special-Purpose Sheds

■ This lakeside shed has a picturesque perch along a path leading down to the water. The shed stows boating and fishing gear.

The previous sections on wood, tool, storage, and garden sheds cover many popular shed applications but by no means all of them. In fact, there's almost no limit to the uses to which you can put a shed—or to the custom designs you can have worked up to suit just about any need or desire.

Wood shop sheds keep the mess, noise, and dust of a woodworking hobby away from the house—and large shed doors simplify the jobs of bringing in lumber and moving out finished projects. Studio sheds offer the artists in the family a place of their own to paint, sculpt, sew, quilt, or follow their muses in just about any medium or discipline. One shed manufacturer even offers a "writer's retreat," complete with a loft bed for creativity-restoring naps, a porch for drinking in natural inspiration—and, oh yes, a built-in desk for actually putting words on paper. Office sheds allow at-home workers the

benefit of a few steps' commute to a space of their own, allowing them to isolate themselves from the distractions of home—and to leave office cares in a separate building at the end of the workday. Guest sheds give you a place to accommodate visitors while preserving privacy—both theirs and yours. Retreat sheds offer a place apart to retreat, meditate, or just take some time for yourself.

Sometimes a shed's main purpose is to adorn the landscape. "We just like looking at it" is a comment frequently made by satisfied owners, and it's a perfectly valid reason for having one.

On the pages that follow, you'll see examples of special-purpose sheds to spark your fancy: a pool shed, a screen room, a retreat, and a few waterside sheds. Some were designed from the ground up to suit a specific purpose or location, but most were clever adaptations of storage or garden shed designs.

HOBBY HAVEN

▲ A few well-considered changes morphed a stock storage shed into a custom retreat for a model aircraft hobbyist.

Here's a handsome backyard retreat that caters to its owner's radio-controlled model airplane hobby. The owner and the building's designer/builder worked together to modify a storage shed design to suit the owner's purpose. They started by raising the roof slightly, creating a handsome, dormered appearance. Next came a custom Dutch door located near the gable end, allowing for the feature the owner wanted most: a large window along the front wall. A small deck affords a place to sit outside; inside, a long antique

workbench provides a spacious, day-lit work area with a view of the backyard and gardens.

The building is nicely detailed with board-and-batten siding, architectural shingles, and copper flashing above the door that directs rainwater away from the doorway. A woodshed extension around back provides a dry spot to store yard and gardening tools and equipment. As a finishing touch, an antique airplane propeller tucked under the dormer eave offers a clue as to what's inside.

One of the benefits of completely sketching

out every detail in advance is an interior that makes use of every square inch yet feels light and spacious even when crammed with tools, model aircraft in various stages of assembly, equipment and memorabilia. The owner insulated the shed and installed a small air conditioner and gas heater for year-round comfort. Lots of adjustable shelving, a pegboard-faced wall, and home-center storage cabinets keep things organized. Ceiling-hung shelf brackets store plane wings and fuselages. Simple pendent lamp fixtures hang low enough so that stored items don't cast shadows; the fixtures also keep the floor and walls uncluttered by lamps. The space even includes a computer weather station to monitor flying conditions and a TV for entertainment when storms ground the pilot's recreational flights.

▶ A hardwood floor and tongue-and-groove pine walls and ceiling add a warm quality to this retreat; gas heat and full insulation keep it toasty in cool weather. Open storage makes things easy to find and allows the colorful models to remain on display when not in use.

POOL SHED

Pools and sheds are great combinations. Pool sheds come in all sizes and can serve a variety of functions. At minimum, a closet-sized shed can cover the pool filtration machinery and store chemicals and cleaning equipment. Somewhat larger sheds also can accommodate the necessary pool covers and water toys.

Make it still larger, and you'll have enough room to store poolside furniture including, perhaps, a picnic table and grill.

The spacious and elegant structure shown here performs all these functions, plus it adds the amenities of a screened area for relaxing or entertaining, a sink and bar, bathroom and shower facilities, a couple of changing rooms, and controls for the poolside stereo system.

A deluxe pool shed such as this one has an important hidden benefit: It allows you to locate the pool without regard to proximity to your house, opening up many more pool-siting possibilities. It also keeps the water, noise, and wear and tear of poolside activities away from the main residence.

■ With its back to the woods and its large, screened porch facing the pool, this handsome shed adds to the pool's sense of enclosure and seclusion. The nearby grill and all the outdoor furniture store in the porch during the off-season.

◀ Inside, a bar counter and sink face the screened openings from the back wall. Changing rooms are to the right as you enter the shed. A sliding door opens wide to allow a caterer with trays easy access and allows the door to be left open without swinging in the wind. A shower fixture is mounted on the gable end opposite the porch for quick rinse-offs after swimming.

▲ "Shed" needn't mean "shabby." As befits a primary entertaining area for a private estate, attention to detail and premium materials abound here. The roof is covered with cedar shingles, gutters and downspouts are copper; sconce lighting provides the patio with a soft glow after sundown; and a hand-wrought bell summons bathers to a picnic meal cooked on the nearby grill.

▲ Pool equipment is tucked under an overhang behind the shed, outside the pool enclosure, allowing the building's interior to be used for living space, service areas, and storage. A gate and path allow easy access for maintenance chores. The shed's materials, color scheme, and even rooflines match those on the main house, seen in the background.

RUSTIC RETREAT

This invitingly rustic retreat serves many functions for its owners, who live in the Green Mountains of southern Vermont. It offers cozy, year-round guest accommodations (a wood stove keeps the interior toasty for ski-season company). When guests are gone, it's a great getaway for the owners, who can read, relax, nap, or just sit on the porch, enjoying the mountain views and tranquility. The building could serve equally well as a year-round office or studio.

The building rests on skids, which were placed on leveled concrete blocks. A false stone

▲ A cross-gabled roof with an entry archway shows off the deep red salvaged entry door. Asymmetrical landscaping and plumb-but-curving porch columns add quirky charm to the building's simple symmetry. Large salvaged windows are divided with muntins, preserving a sense of scale. Identical windows in back create a light-filled interior with through-views that make the shed seem far larger than it really is.

foundation, built of rocks gathered on-site, gives the building a look of permanence. The stone-edged, raised flower bed helps disguise the grade change under the building and adds color.

Constructed entirely of rough-sawn native

lumber, this shed features random-width board-and-batten pine siding and hemlock framing. All exposed wood was left to weather naturally; a durable metal roof adds a board-and-batten-like striated texture to the roof.

Several elements add up to give this structure a storybook cottage appeal. They include:

salvaged windows and doors, antique lace curtains, art glass wall inserts, and peeled hemlock porch columns. The whole building has a sort of organic, funky, one-of-a-kind charm that makes you want to leave the rest of life behind for a while and move in.

▲ The opposite gable has a bay window cantilevered out from the building's side on diagonal braces. The tiny bump-out adds a built-in seating nook to the living room. A small, handblown art glass window is set in the bump-out's side.

▲ Another salvaged window, this one on the rear bearing wall, sports its original wavy glass and peeling black paint. Extreme variations in the width of the rough-sawn pine boards used in the siding add a random, organic character and rich texture to the exterior.

SCREEN ROOM

Halfway between a gazebo and a shed lies the screen room, a sort of detached porch that you can plunk down anywhere on your property. They're traditionally called "summer houses" in New England, whence this example hails. Its builder refers to it as a "Florida room." No matter what you call them, they're a great feature, especially in buggy regions where an open, unscreened gazebo would allow mosquitoes to drive you and your guests indoors. And, because such structures are screened on four sides, they offer terrific cross ventilation and 360-degree views.

Screen rooms can be used as outdoor entertainment and dining pavilions beside pools, on decks and patios, in gardens, and beside water features such as ponds or fountains. They're great for entertaining drop-by guests and neighbors without having to invite them indoors: Simply bring out a pitcher of lemonade and relax. Some screen house owners

▼ A green metal roof blends with this site's lawn and foliage. The eaves overhang the siding for a handsome look that's also practical: The overhangs help keep the interior of the room dry and moisture off of the rough-sawn siding.

▲ Offered as an accessory, this Adirondack rocker complements the screen room's interior. Several building manufacturers offer accessories—ranging from furniture to hardware—specially designed to complement their buildings.

stash a small refrigerator and cabinet of glasses in their structure so they're always ready if unexpected guests show up.

Built of rough-sawn pine, this one features a unique fan detail over the entryway. Double doors are wide enough to allow a large picnic table or outdoor seating pieces to pass easily. Large screened panels on the upper parts of the doors create an unobstructed view; smaller panels below can be easily replaced if a foot (or exuberant pet) accidentally tears the screen.

▶ This screen room was an impulse buy for the owner, who saw it on display and realized he had the perfect site for it: on a terraced hillside overlooking a meadow. The gracefully curving stone wall, however, prevented the delivery truck from backing up to the site, so the completed building was set in place using a crane. Owners of even more difficult sites have resorted to helicopters to place buildings in the precise location they desire.

PATHS AND WALKWAYS

LAWN

▲ Plunk down your building at any convenient spot on your lawn.

■ **Pros:** Sometimes the best treatment is no treatment at all. And what could be easier?

■ **Tip:** If you own a side-discharge mower, face the discharge chute away from the building when you mow. Grass-blasted siding looks tacky, and is very difficult to clean. Similarly, take care with your string trimmer; repeated whipping can erode softwood siding.

STEPPING-STONES

▶ Buy stepping-stones at your local home center, lay them out in a path that's convenient and good-looking, and set them into your lawn.

■ **Pros:** This inexpensive, fast-installing option stands up to heavy foot traffic and adds a pleasing element of hardscape to your lawn.

■ **Tip:** For a neat, level installation, place the steppers where you want them, then slice into the sod around them with a spade or shovel. Remove each stone, take out the sod and soil beneath it to the same depth as the stone, and set the stone in place.

The approach to your building's entry is important, both practically and aesthetically. You want a surface that'll stand up to the traffic, looks good, and is easy to maintain. Fortunately, you have many choices. Here are a few examples, roughly in order of complexity:

GRASS PATH

▲ Plant a strip of lawn leading to your shed.

■ **Pros:** Good-looking, soft underfoot, and easy to maintain, grass paths are an inexpensive, oft-overlooked option. Because paths concentrate traffic, you need to take a few precautions that wouldn't be required if you chose the lawn option above left. First, make sure the soil beneath the path is reasonably well-drained. Second, avoid repeatedly subjecting the surface to heavy loads that can cause ruts.

■ **Tip:** Don't just scatter any old grass seed— get stuff that's rated for heavy traffic and for the light conditions (full sun, partial sun, or shade) that the path's location offers.

FLAGSTONE-AND-GRAVEL PATH

◀ Excavate a path a few inches deep, line it with landscape fabric, fill it with gravel, and lay flagstones on top. Or use pea gravel, which is more comfortable to walk on than larger gravels, and forgo the flagstones.

■ **Pros:** If the soil in front of your shed is poorly drained, heavily shaded, or both, a living pathway will turn into dust or mud quickly. This natural, informal-looking alternative involves some expense and heavy lifting but helps ensure firm, dry footing.

■ **Tip:** To prevent the gravel from scattering, dig the path several inches wider than the walkway and edge it with cobbles as shown. The edging looks great, too.

BRICK PATH

▲ Excavate and lay landscape fabric as above for a gravel path, but cover it with sand, then lay bricks on top.

■ **Pros:** Red brick contrasts nicely with green foliage, and you can choose from many patterns. All have a less organic, more formal character than flagstone or gravel. They offer a surface that's more uniform and on which it's easier to maneuver wheeled equipment.

■ **Tip:** After laying the bricks, dust the top of the path with sand and brush it into the cracks for a look that rivals that of a mortared walkway.

RAMP

▲ Build a sloping runway in front of the shed out of a smooth-surfaced material such as pressure-treated decking or pavers.

■ **Pros:** Wheeled equipment such as lawn mowers, garden tractors, wheelbarrows, and garbage bins will glide in and out. So can bicycles, tricycles, wagons, and other yard toys, making it easy for kids to put away what they haul out. A properly constructed ramp makes the building easily accessible to people of any age or ability, and the smooth surface is easy to clear of ice and snow.

■ **Tip:** Make the ramp long enough so the slope is gentle. If you're building the ramp of wood, run the boards across the direction of travel to increase traction. If you use decking screws, set them slightly below the surface so they don't snag on shovels and your snowblower's tire chains in winter. If your ramp gets a lot of use or you live in a location with significant rainfall, allow for drainage at the base to avoid creating a mud puddle, and consider adding a small masonry pad there, as shown, to minimize erosion.

GAZEBOS

Gazebos offer a wonderful perch for savoring your outdoor environment. These little (and sometimes not so little) self-contained structures can be sited just about anywhere, giving you a chance to escape your house in favor of fresh air and picturesque vistas. ("Gazebo" is a shortening and combining of the two words "gaze about.")

But gazebos offer so much more: At their best, gazebos are lovely architectural gems, designed as much to be looked at as they are to be looked out of. And as you'll see on the following pages, they can solve a plethora of design and practical challenges:

■ These relatively simple, affordable structures can add personality to a featureless yard.

■ On rugged terrain, they offer a vantage point from an otherwise inaccessible location, serving as a resting point for both the eyes and the legs.

■ Compared to most decks, gazebos provide more utility and protection.

■ What structure has more potential to define a series of outdoor rooms? A gazebo can welcome visitors to your woodland, serve as an outdoor dining pavilion when entertaining, and add beauty to your garden.

You may need a toolshed, but by the time you finish this section, you'll probably want a gazebo, too.

▼ **This gazebo with its peaked roof and lattice-embellished sides complements the formal garden landscape that surrounds it.**

▲ This classic cedar gazebo—complete with wood shingle roof, cupola, and Victorian-style bracketing—offers a contemplative resting place in a backyard glade.

INSTANT INTEREST

While gazebos are quite at home in established landscapes, they're also an excellent way to add instant personality to a yard in a new development, where trees and other plantings will take time to mature. The gazebos on these pages were installed in new developments where the homeowners started from the tabula rasa of a yard that sported lots of green turf–and little else.

Adding a gazebo can create a focal point that draws the eye away from the monolith of a new house on flat ground, adding height and mass elsewhere in the yard to balance, compose, and frame the view. A gazebo also adds an outlying destination, giving visitors and homeowners alike a reason to venture across the sea of green to a secluded getaway. Gazebo-inspired paths and plantings can add further character, color, and composition to the blank canvas of a new yard.

Victorian folly

This gazebo crowns a short walk in the side yard of a new landscape. The approach to the gazebo unwinds pleasantly beside mounds of boxwood hedge and miniature roses. Because the structure is often viewed through a rose-entangled arbor at the driveway, decorative metal brackets on the gazebo repeat the motif. This gazebo was built on concrete piers with 4×6 and 2×6 pressure-treated lumber and topped with cedar shakes. Fascia boards are 1×6. The structure was painted after assembly.

Room with a view

Perhaps the biggest benefit of a gazebo is that it

▲ This 10-foot-wide gazebo offers homeowners and guests alike a secluded destination in a new yard.

gives you the freedom to put a "room" almost anywhere. This lakeside gazebo in a yard in a new development features a simple, square design to maximize the view: There are a minimum of posts and no railings to obscure the lake vista, whether it's viewed from inside or outside the gazebo.

The simple structure is deceptively well-

equipped, however. It includes a ceiling fan, a light, and stereo speakers, all controlled from inside the house. A stepping-stone path draws you to it, and benches (backless to allow maximum lake view) invite you to sit and rest a while.

The gazebo was constructed of pressure-treated pine wrapped in spruce, then sealed and painted. It tops a concrete pad and has an asphalt shingle roof that matches that of the house.

Double duty

Even a small gazebo can have a big effect. The 6½-foot-wide structure at right does double duty, offering both a great getaway at the edge of a wooded area and a view back toward the elaborately landscaped house. Actually, one could say that the structure has a third function as an armature on which to hang planters. The plants fill the gazebo with color and fragrance, and ivy flows off a lattice "wall" and across the flagstone floor.

▲ Serving as a perch for plants as well as people, this small gazebo anchors fragrant and attractive plantings both alow and aloft.

UPSLOPE, DOWNSLOPE

A gazebo can help transform unused, steeply sloping backyard areas into charming, private spaces for entertaining and leisure. That's especially true if a gazebo is combined with other features, such as terraced garden beds, paths with steps, elevated decks, or sunken patios. Here are some examples:

Take the high road

The raised retreat below left provides its owners with views of their swimming pool on one side and of the surrounding woods and a small pond on the other. Attractive terracing unifies the gazebo, a broad series of steps, a bench, and garden beds into one attractive composition; the angular beds mimic the lines of the hexagonal gazebo's design. At night, path-side lighting leads visitors to the structure. The gazebo's screen panels and door assure bug-free evening gatherings there.

Nice landing!

Far below this Oregon home, the blue Willamette River rushes by. But this soothing scene was formerly unreachable due to a steep pitch and a thicket of scrub. A gazebo was the solution, combined with paths that snake to its location: an elegant midpoint landing. A bridge, patio, and waterfall further embellish the area.

The 8-foot-high cedar gazebo affords the owners both river and woodland views, as well as a welcome resting place when they make the arduous climb from the water's edge. The 12-foot-diameter structure also offers shelter from sudden rains—an important consideration in a location some distance from the house.

◄ Following a trail of brightly colored flowers by day and low-voltage path lighting by night leads you to this ridgetop gazebo with a double view of a swimming pool on one side and a pond on the other.

▲ Often, a gazebo in a remote location such as this becomes the focus of its own little landscape. Here, a stacked-stone retaining wall piles naturally into the woodland setting, a bridge arches the stream, and a fire pit recessed into the gravel terrace adds special appeal to a gazebo visit on crisp fall evenings.

◄ Ornamental iron brackets between the posts and rafters give this gazebo Victorian charm. Ironwork repeats in the arched bridge that spans a small stream below the garden's constructed waterfall.

A solution "up-piers"

Here, a bridge tames a hillside, leading to a gazebo built on piers above a river floodplain. Not only is the structure safe from seasonal flooding on its elevated foundation, it also offers a better view of the river behind it. The simple, square structure is embellished with a latticelike tracery that adds visual interest without impeding the view, as would true lattice. The motif is repeated in the bridge railings. Construction was but little more complex than it would have been had the building been lower to the ground—longer corner posts provide the necessary height, while diagonal bracing keeps the taller uprights vertical and stiffens the floor.

▲ Chippendale-style latticework adds architectural character to the railings and sides of this gazebo without impeding the view, as traditional crisscross lattice would.

PERCH, DON'T PLUNGE

▶ **Does the site make the gazebo, or the gazebo make the site? Much of the fun in owning a gazebo is deciding precisely where to place it—both to punctuate the landscape when viewed from afar and to frame the view when looking outward from the structure. This one was placed to mediate the relationship between a grand vista and an intimate garden.**

With your eyes focused on the green valleys and hilly vistas in the background, you could easily tumble down a steep hill and right into a stream and pond, were it not for a railing that encourages you to pause at this ridgetop gazebo. The structure offers an intimate frame for the nearly overwhelming view. Hand-split cedar shakes help the simple structure's roof blend into its environment, while white-painted uprights and railings offer a crisp contrast to the surrounding green.

On the borderline

A barren and uninspiring rectangular tract, this yard had an unusable slope as its only focal point. Filled with weeds and too steep to mow, the hill was an eyesore. The tall, white-painted gazebo transformed the yard, masking the slope and providing a focal point that offered a more pleasing perch for the eye. A grove of citrus trees planted behind it forms an attractive green background that contrasts nicely with the white structure. A flower border along the bottom of the slope is filled to overflowing and a brick stepping-stone path leads to the shady retreat.

◀ This gazebo functions as a focal point in the flower border, drawing the eye away from a domineering slope.

LANDSCAPING A GAZEBO

A gazebo promises romantic escapes, but only if landscaping aids in the effect. Fortunately, a little landscaping goes a long way when it comes to gazebos. For visual balance, landscaping should flow out from the gazebo at least the distance of the structure's width— more if you choose landscaping that lacks trees, arbors, or other tall counterbalances to the gazebo. Simpler designs, such as gazebos without cupolas or sides, have a see-through effect and melt more quickly into the landscape. A backdrop such as a hedge or fence can make the structure stand out a bit more.

▲ Preformed brick stepping-stones, available at landscape and home centers, make an elegant and economical pathway that's also easy to install.

DECK THE DECK

Decks are dandy, but if you want porchlike protection from the elements without being tied to your house, a deck-top gazebo can't be beat.

Golf-course gazebo

Situated to provide a bug-free retreat after an alfresco meal, this gazebo also offers great golf-course views.

The deck-and-gazebo combo also improves the appearance of this home as seen from the backyard or beyond. The tall walls and high roofline of the house initially towered over the yard, and the back door sat several steps above ground level. In response, the deck was designed to ease the transition in height—and add some foreground interest—by winding down two levels to the lawn.

The white-painted trimwork of the upper

▼ This design proves that you can build a gazebo in close proximity to your house—if you take care to make use of similar materials, colors, and details on both structures.

▲ The bug screens on this gazebo also offer some protection from errant golf balls, so when some hacker yells, "Fore!" you don't have to duck.

deck and gazebo matches that of the house, and the gazebo shares similar rooflines and the same roofing material as the house—moves that tie gazebo, deck, and house into a single harmonious composition. In addition, the lower deck repeats the gazebo's octagonal shape.

Inspired integration

The grand gazebo at left acts as a hub that joins the spokes of this home's porches and terraces with the house itself.

Located at the end of a terrace staging down from the house, this structure's fieldstone foundation is tied in to the terrace wall. The aggregate concrete of the terrace was also used for the gazebo floor, making it seem like a room of the house—but with a getaway feeling.

Instead of a more traditional cupola, the gazebo is topped by a stained-glass finial inspired by the setting sun, which appears to get larger and change color as it settles into the

▲ This 13½-foot-wide gazebo provides space for built-in benches and a small dining table.

▲ The arched openings frame a living painting of live oaks and a valley vista beyond.

horizon. The finial's opalescent glass inserts go from silvery white to amber to rosy red, mimicking the western sky at sunset.

Triple treat

Here, a gazebo, deck, and patio combine to create a luxurious suite of outdoor rooms fit for both intimate family gatherings and entertaining large crowds. Railing and shingle styles, materials selection, and trim colors unite the three areas. The gazebo is strategically placed to balance the mass of the house, punctuate the end of the deck, and offer a sense of enclosure to the whole area.

When bugs appear, gatherings can retreat from the patio's wicker-furnished fire-pit area to the screen gazebo. At night, a combination of recessed step lighting, deck-mounted lanterns, and accent lighting on the gazebo's eaves and interior provides decorative, mood, and safety lighting for the entire area.

▲ A gazebo combines nicely with a deck and patio to provide a suite of outdoor living spaces.

GARDEN GRACE

A garden is a natural place for a gazebo. The little buildings can add welcome structure to a garden's organic forms, provide a destination for garden paths, offer a place to sit and admire the view, and provide shade and a measure of weather protection for garden entertaining.

A thicket of underbrush on uneven ground used to inhabit the corner of this wooded yard, where the gazebo now perches. No more! Fieldstone retaining walls and a flagstone path make the area accessible while adding to its character. A rushing stream runs through the area, bridged by a walkway set into the path.

Planning around her use of a wheelchair, the owner finds that the combination of a smooth pathway and raised beds allows easy access to this area, both for garden maintenance and relaxation in the gazebo.

▲ Built of the traditional choice of unfinished cedar, this gazebo will naturally weather to a gray color that will blend in nicely with the surrounding tree trunks. A path makes this formerly inaccessible thicket a pleasant getaway.

▶ A garden-enclosed water feature, such as this rock-rimmed lily pond, offers an ideal location for a gazebo.

CAMPED IN A CLEARING

Sometimes a sunny clearing needs a bit of shade and a structure to give the area a focal point. This engaging gazebo is located in the clearing at the bottom of a wooded valley.

Separated from the main yard by a tree-covered slope and path, this site needed something to connect it to the rest of the property—both for visual harmony and to politely announce that the land was private. The owners also wanted to be able to linger by the stream to read and relax.

This gazebo was the answer. Sporting the same color scheme, traditional style, and materials as the house, it visually unites the intervale with the main house and yard while standing out smartly against the forested backdrop. The rushing brook close by makes it a favorite spot for reading, sitting, conversing with friends, or enjoying a glass of iced tea.

Because the area around the gazebo is shaded by tree-covered slopes, this custom-designed structure features a skylight of clear acrylic panels set into the hexagonal roof peak to bathe the interior with light.

▲ **Plants and climbing roses naturally tie this gazebo to the landscape. Instead of standing out, it becomes part of the garden.**

▶ **This streamside gazebo offers a great excuse to while away a summer afternoon with a book and a glass of iced tea. Wicker furnishings complement the vintage design—and are lightweight and easy to carry back to the main house at the end of the season.**

LUXURIOUS LIGHTING

Illumination enhances a gazebo's usefulness after the sun sets. Electric outdoor lighting converts inky shadows into inviting living areas. What's more, lighting ensures sure footing and increases your yard's security.

To cast a welcoming glow, choose low-voltage lighting to bathe a gazebo or shed area with gentle illumination. You can find easy-to-install low-voltage lighting kits at home centers and hardware stores and on the Internet. Install

▶ **For dramatic effect, use strands of lights to outline your gazebo's eaves and ceiling lights to illuminate its handsome roof structure.**

A gazebo built for entertaining should span at least 10 feet, and should provide at least 75 inches of headroom. This porchlike screen gazebo also features overhead lighting for evening dining and potted plants that bring the garden right inside.

light-sensitive photocell timers to switch lights on and off automatically at dusk and dawn. Instead of lighting all areas uniformly, use a variety of fixtures with different angles of light, such as dramatic uplighting and traditional downlighting. Arrange illumination around your gazebo to create patches of light and shadow. Plan your lighting for easy light bulb changing. Install a switch in the house for convenient control of your landscape lights.

▶ For safety and security, tuck lights beside paths, into stair-step risers, and near outdoor seating. Include some strong-beam lights to discourage intruders.

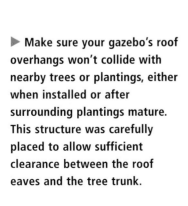

▶ Make sure your gazebo's roof overhangs won't collide with nearby trees or plantings, either when installed or after surrounding plantings mature. This structure was carefully placed to allow sufficient clearance between the roof eaves and the tree trunk.

DETAILS, DETAILS, DETAILS

Whether you're building a gazebo or a shed, the final effect will be the result of a broad collection of decisions. Here are some you might want to consider as you go about choosing, detailing, and assembling your outbuilding.

Fasteners

Start with the nitty-gritty. What holds your building together is important—and not just for its structural integrity. The wrong kind of fasteners can not only loosen but also can stain and discolor your building or even cause rot and decay over time. If you're building your shed or gazebo yourself, see the information on fasteners on page 146–147 to help you make a good choice. If you're buying a panelized or prebuilt shed or gazebo, read on.

◀ Ideally, exposed nails in siding and trim should be hand-nailed, and the nails should be driven so the heads are just flush with the surface, both for a neat appearance and to avoid damaging the wood.

▲ Look closely at how the fasteners were driven. Using a pneumatic framing nailer on siding can result in a nailhead sunk deep beneath the surface of the wood. Using nailers speeds up production and keeps costs down, but the result can look bad—particularly if the nails weren't placed precisely and symmetrically. More important, overdriven nails leave a depression in the wood that allows water to penetrate and rot to start.

▲ Machine-driven steel staples like the one shown here start rusting fast, discoloring the wood. Eventually, they can even rust through, causing your shed to fall apart like a house of cards. If you're buying a panelized or pre-built shed, look for one constructed with rust-resistant fasteners that are either triple-dip galvanized or stainless steel to ensure you won't have problems later on. Plated fasteners—the type used in most air nailers—don't hold up nearly as well.

Hardware

Building hardware–hinges, door handles, latches, and more–can make a big difference in the appearance, durability, and ease of use of your structure. Here's an overview of popular hardware choices:

Salvage

There's nothing wrong with using salvage hardware, especially if you're using salvage lumber, windows, doors, or other secondhand materials. Just make sure you use something robust and long lasting enough to do the job.

▲ This old-but-sturdy strap hinge is plenty strong to handle the door on a small toolshed, and its rusty patina blends well with the recycled barn board of the shed and door. It's fastened to the door with gold-tone screws that add gemlike sparkle to the old hardware.

▲ If you can't find vintage hardware, make your own. This toolshed handle is fashioned from an old leather strap screwed securely to the door.

▲ For centuries, simple, hand-hewn wood latches and handles like this pair helped open doors and keep them shut. Such wooden "hardware" is easy to make out of scrap lumber.

▲ An old brass cabinet latch complements weathered siding. Flea markets and junk shops can be great sources of vintage hardware. Resist the urge to clean up such finds—they'll match the character of your shed better if you use them just as they are.

■ **New.** If you're building your shed yourself, you can choose the hardware. If you're buying it as a package or completed unit from a manufacturer, you still may have choices. Ask about the hardware that comes with the package before buying to make sure it's what you want. If not, ask about upgrades—or special order your own hardware.

■ **None.** Sometimes the best hardware is no hardware at all.

▲ Heavy-duty steel hinges such as this one are a good choice for shed doors. This one is securely fastened to the doorjamb and the thickest part of the door with big lag screws.

▲ Plated gate latches such as this are inexpensive, strong, functional, and bored for heavy-duty fasteners. They're either sadly utilitarian or barnyard chic, depending on your point of view.

▲ This handsome, vintage-style hinge is also long on security: No fewer than eight wood screws secure it to the door frame; the strap gets a carriage bolt and two more wood screws.

▲ Sliding bolt latches such as this allow doors to be secured both top and bottom for an extra-secure closure. They're often used on one side of a double-door—the side that you close first and latch from the inside.

▲ Brass is a top-drawer choice for decorative hardware, such as this newel post on a gazebo railing. Just keep in mind that the metal, like the cedar post it's mounted to, will acquire a mellow patina over time. Compare the two photos for a sense of how the material looks when new and after a few seasons of weathering.

◀ This window system is simply a multipaned wooden-sashed unit set in a frame. Pegs set into boards fastened to the window framing allow the sash to be tipped back slightly for ventilation while preventing rain from blowing in. The window can also be removed altogether for maximum airflow. There's no hinge to loosen or fail, no sliding sash to swell and stick. Ingenious!

SHED AND GAZEBO PROJECTS

Now that you've sampled the range of sheds and gazebos, you may wonder how much time, skill, and site preparation it takes to build them. This chapter presents four projects; each features a different approach to building. You'll find a woodshed of rough-sawn lumber, a gazebo of dimension lumber, a garden shed built from a precut kit, and a potting shed built from a panelized kit.

These four projects give you a sense of what's involved in each approach so you can choose which method is right for you. In each case, you'll see a photograph of the completed building, an illustration of how the pieces fit together, and lists of the materials and tools required to do the job. An illustrated overview of the entire building process shows you what needs to be done. With the exception of the gazebo project, these overviews are not intended to guide the construction of a hands-on project. However, plans and/or kits are available from the manufacturers of all three sheds. See the buying guide on page 170 for more information.

BUILDING A
WOODSHED

▲ **Rough-sawn lumber and a classic design make this a sturdy, handsome, and functional woodshed. This example is painted and covered with a metal roof.**

This 4×10-foot woodshed is a good place to start if you've not constructed a building before. Its small size and relative simplicity provide a nice introduction to the building process.

Materials

This particular shed was designed to be built from rough-sawn lumber. Using rough-sawn stock has several advantages:

■ Because it's not planed, finished, graded, or treated—and because you're buying it directly from the mill—rough-sawn wood is less expensive than the smooth-planed stock you find at lumberyards.

■ It's also more robust, as its actual and nominal dimensions are the same: A rough-sawn 2×4 actually measures 2 inches by 4 inches rather than the 1½×3½ inches of nominal 2×4 planed lumber. These beefy timbers give buildings extra strength that's nice to have if you're storing heavy stuff, such as the split firewood this shed was designed to house.

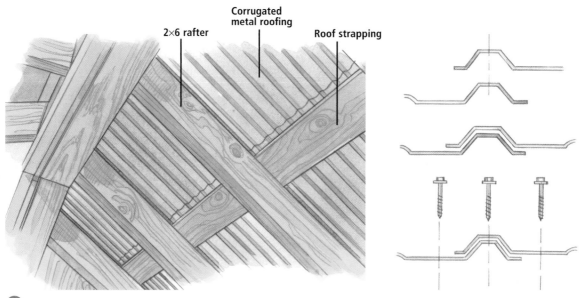

2×6 rafter

Corrugated
metal roofing

Roof strapping

④ Use rubber-gasketed wood screws, shown in detail, to attach the overlapped corrugated metal roofing to the roof strapping.

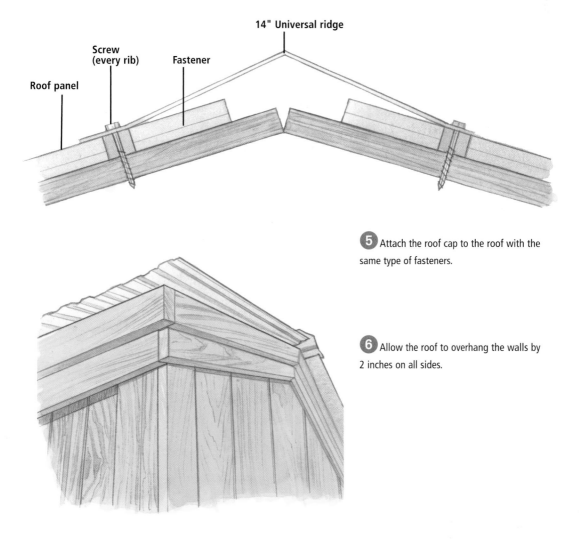

14" Universal ridge

Screw
(every rib)

Fastener

Roof panel

⑤ Attach the roof cap to the roof with the same type of fasteners.

⑥ Allow the roof to overhang the walls by 2 inches on all sides.

BUILDING A
GARDEN SHED

This elegant garden shed can serve many purposes: potting shed, studio, office, retreat, guest cottage, pool cabana, or storage shed. The options are limited only by the owner's imagination.

This structure is a substantial project, especially if it is to be built on a concrete slab foundation. In fact, with the exception of plumbing and insulation, it's almost like building a small house.

Fortunately, this building is available as either a precut lumber kit or a panelized kit, (sometimes referred to as a "preassembled kit) substantially simplifying its construction. If you

order the precut a kit, you'll get a large, neatly wrapped package or two, mounted on pallets and delivered to your location by truck. Inside are all the materials required to build the structure. All the dimension lumber is precut and marked for installation. The fasteners and hardware, siding, roofing, windows, and doors also may be included. The panelized kit goes a step further, supplying framed and sided walls. The project shown here and on the following pages was built from the more labor-intensive precut lumber kit. Such a kit is less expensive than a panelized kit, and more easily transported to a remote or confined site.

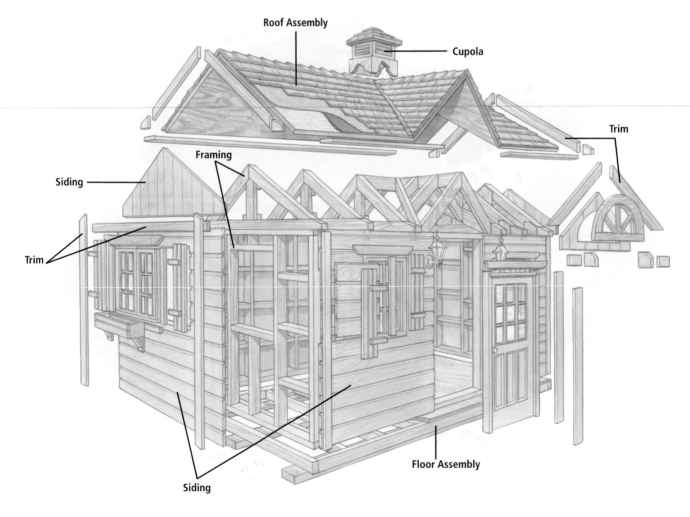

MATERIALS

BUILDING KIT

CONCRETE FOR

FOUNDATION

TOOLS:

HAMMER

TAPE MEASURE

CIRCULAR SAW

HANDSAW OR

RECIPROCATING SAW

DRILL-DRIVER

½" DRILL BIT

UTILITY KNIFE

CARPENTER'S LEVEL

FRAMING SQUARE

ADJUSTABLE WRENCH

½" WOOD CHISEL

CHALK LINE

▲ Assembled, trimmed, landscaped, and finished, the kit has been transformed into an elegant garden shed.

Because the kit contains only what you'll need, you'll have hardly any waste material to dispose of, and you'll need just a few basic tools.

The steps presented here will give you a pretty good idea of the nature of the project, which will take a moderately skilled do-it-yourselfer and a helper a week to complete (allow a few days more for the installation of the concrete pad foundation, depending on site conditions). Because these steps rely on the use of kit parts not specified here, they won't guide you in the construction of an actual building.

However, similar instructions are found with kit buildings available from a number of manufacturers. If in doubt as to what's supplied in a kit, ask to see a list of the package contents and a sample set of instructions before ordering. (Some manufacturers allow you to download sample instructions from their website.) For more on how to choose a building kit package, see pages 134–135.

BUILD THE CONCRETE FOUNDATION

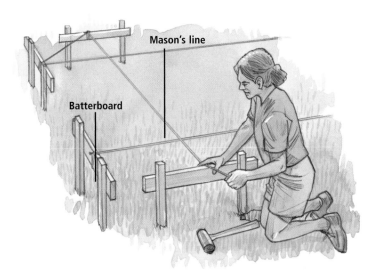

1 Use stakes, batterboards, and string to mark the foundation's outline. Be sure the string is straight and level.

2 Excavate the topsoil and replace it with a gravel or sand bed. Rent a vibrating compactor to compress the material after digging and again after adding bed material.

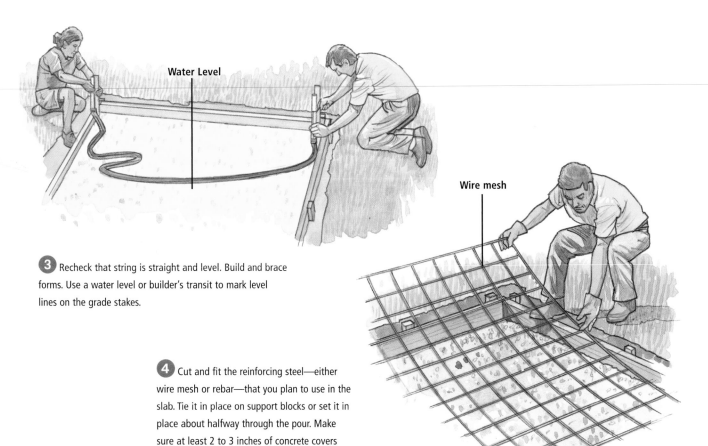

3 Recheck that string is straight and level. Build and brace forms. Use a water level or builder's transit to mark level lines on the grade stakes.

4 Cut and fit the reinforcing steel—either wire mesh or rebar—that you plan to use in the slab. Tie it in place on support blocks or set it in place about halfway through the pour. Make sure at least 2 to 3 inches of concrete covers the steel.

2×4 screed

5 Dampen the substrate, then start the pour. If possible, get the concrete truck's chute directly over the forms so you don't have to transport the concrete in batches. Keep the chute end low and moving to distribute the concrete evenly.

6 Use a straight 2×4 or other board as a screed to strike off and level the concrete with the top edges of the forms. A first pass with a tamping motion will help settle any large aggregate that's too close to the surface. Then slide the screed along the forms with a slight side-to-side sawing motion. Fill in any low spots, then run the screed again until the surface is flat and level.

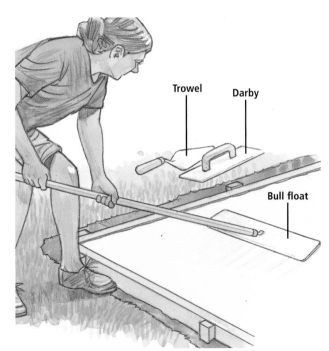

Trowel   Darby

Bull float

Grooving tool

7 Before bleed water appears on the slab's surface, smooth the surface with a hand float or darby for small slabs; for larger slabs use a bull float, which has a handle like a broom. Keep the leading edge of the float slightly elevated and push the tool across the concrete. Make the first float pass perpendicular to the strike-off direction; make a second pass perpendicular to the first. Floating forces large aggregate down and consolidates the surface.

8 If you're including control joints, rough them out now using a groover and a straightedge. Also use a pointed trowel to score along the edges of the forms (to displace the aggregate), then run an edger along the perimeter of the slab. This creates a slightly rounded edge that's less prone to chipping or to causing injury if someone falls on it.

CEMENT PAD FOUNDATION

Acement pad is overkill for many small outbuildings but may be necessary if your floor will be heavily loaded with either wheeled or stationary machinery such as a tractor or woodworking equipment, if your site is ledgy, or if you wish to heat the building with in-floor radiant heating. A cement pad foundation requires a good deal of digging and a substantial amount of concrete, so you may need to hire its construction. If you're laying your own foundation, be prepared to rent some digging, mixing, and concrete-finishing equipment. Or you may already have a slab you can build on—an unused portion of your driveway or patio or perhaps even a slab that outlasted an old garage.

◀ A concrete pad can often be built on difficult sites that rule out the use of less labor-intensive foundations. This site on an uneven rock ledge offered no firm, horizontal surface on which to place a cement block foundation and prevented digging holes for a post foundation. Although the cement slab proved most stable and practical, it involved a lot of hand digging.

▶ If your site is inaccessible to a cement truck with a simple chute, you can order concrete from a supplier that can pump the material from the truck to the site in a hose—an option preferable to transporting the concrete from truck to site in a wheelbarrow.

BUILD THE FLOOR

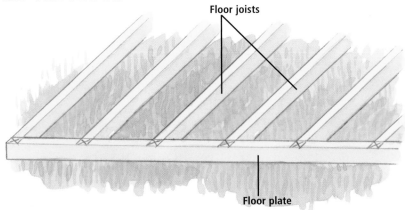

Floor joists

Floor plate

1 Lay the floor out on the slab the way it will be nailed together, lining joists up with the marks on the plates.

2 Using two 3-inch nails for each joint, nail through the plates and into the joists. Ensure that plates and joists are flush at top and bottom.

3 Measure the completed floor's diagonals. If the measurements are the same, your floor is square. If they aren't, push or pull at the corners of the floor until the measurements are the same.

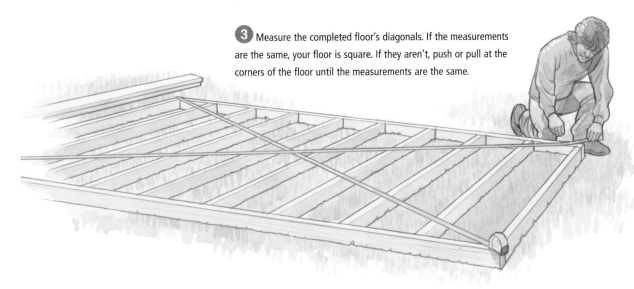

BUILD THE FLOOR (continued)

4 Place pressure-treated 2×6s approximately six inches inside each side. Space any additional runners supplied with your kit evenly across the width of the floor. Nail the runners to the joists with 3-inch nails.

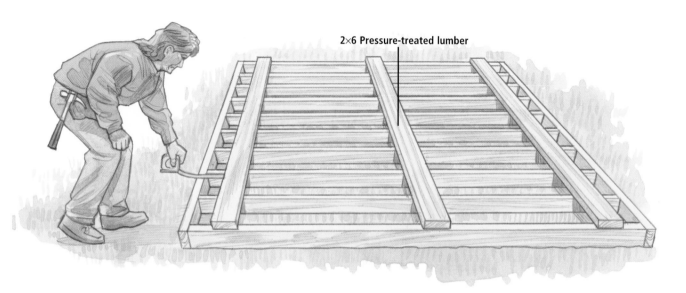

2×6 Pressure-treated lumber

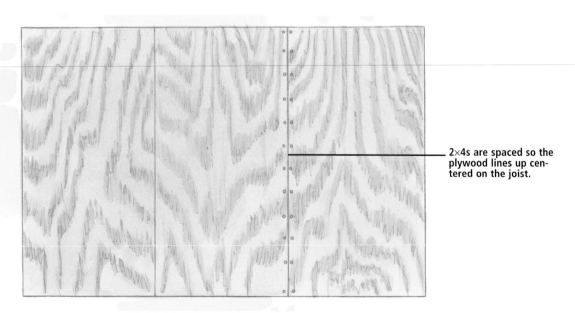

2×4s are spaced so the plywood lines up centered on the joist.

5 Lay plywood sheets over the floor so that the sheets butt against one another directly over a floor joist. Use a chalk line to mark the location of joists on the plywood. Secure the plywood to the joists, spacing nails 8 inches apart along each chalk line and along the edges of each sheet.

BUILD THE WALLS

1 Assemble all the precut wall parts on the newly completed floor. Lay out the plates first. Place studs at the marks provided on each plate. Nail the studs to the plates using 3-inch nails, two nails to each joint. Measure the completed stud wall from corner to corner. As with the floor, adjust the assembly until the measurements are equal.

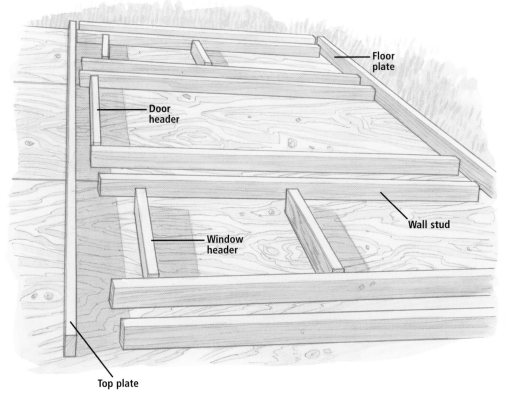

Floor plate

Door header

Wall stud

Window header

Top plate

2 Drive a screw through the wall assembly into the decking at each corner to ensure that the wall remains square while it is being sided.

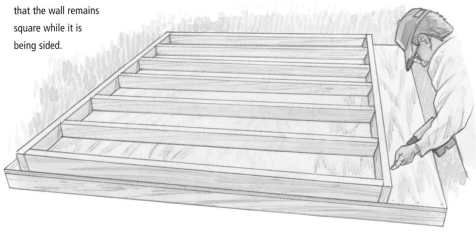

3 Side the walls with the horizontal tongue-and-groove siding provided. (On front and back walls, position siding so that it overhangs the wall by 3½ inches on either side so that when the walls are assembled, the siding will cover the gable-end walls. On gable-end walls, install the siding flush with the studs on either end of the wall.) Use the siding on which the tongue has been cut off for the first course. Place this course with the square side down, overlapping the bottom plate by ¾ inches. Use two 2-inch nails to secure the siding to each stud.

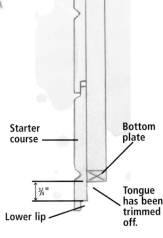

Starter course

Bottom plate

¾"

Lower lip

Tongue has been trimmed off.

BUILD THE WALLS *(continued)*

4 Once the first course is fastened, attach succeeding courses, pulling each course tight to the course beneath it before nailing. Periodically measure the distance between the siding and the top plate on either end of the wall. Adjust siding if necessary to keep the measurements equal.

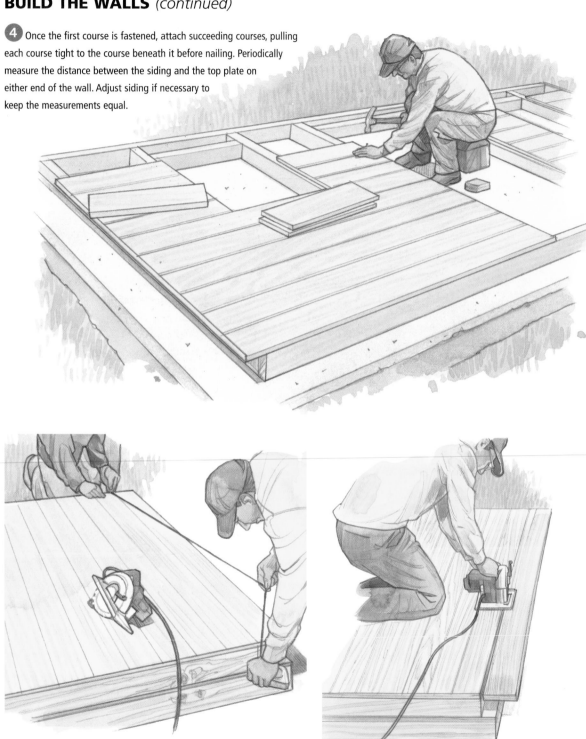

5 Once the top row of siding is nailed in place, use a chalk line to mark the face of the siding along a line flush with the top plate.

6 Using a circular saw, cut the siding along the chalk line.

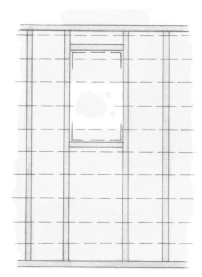

7 Siding for windows and doors will overhang the opening slightly. Cut the siding flush with the openings using a handsaw or reciprocating saw.

8 Place the completed walls around the floor in their proper location. With a helper or two, in the back wall into place. Have your helpers hold it in place while you tip a sidewall into place. Tightly hold or clamp the sidewall flush with the back wall. Secure the two walls together using 3-inch screws placed approximately 8 inches apart. Repeat this procedure with the opposite side wall, then with the front wall.

9 Check the walls for square by measuring diagonals and adjust the walls until the measurements are the same. (Note: the illustrations for steps 8-10 show horizontal siding nailers between studs. These are required if you're installing vertical siding, but you can leave them out if you're using lap siding.)

10 Screw the walls to the floor. Have a helper push the bottom of the wall you're fastening inward, ensuring the wall is tight to the floor but taking care not to knock the wall out of square. Fasten the walls to the floor with 3-inch screws placed approximately every 8 inches.

GABLE ROOF ASSEMBLY

1 Assemble ceiling trusses on a flat surface. Nail them together as shown with three 2-inch nails.

2 Place plywood gussets as shown. Use approximately 12 nails to secure each gusset. Nail the side gussets first, then the peak gusset, then the gusset at the base of the king post.

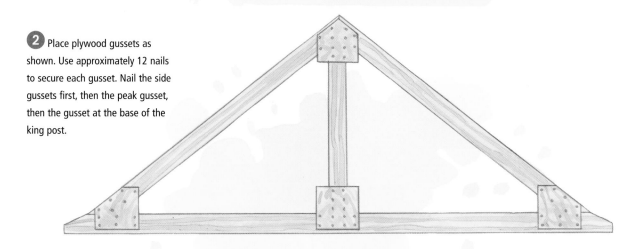

3 Nail siding in place using four 2-inch' nails in each piece. Place nails within ¾ inch of the ends of the siding so that they will be covered by trim when the building is complete. Snug each piece of siding up against the last and use framing square to ensure each piece of siding is perpendicular to the bottom of the truss.

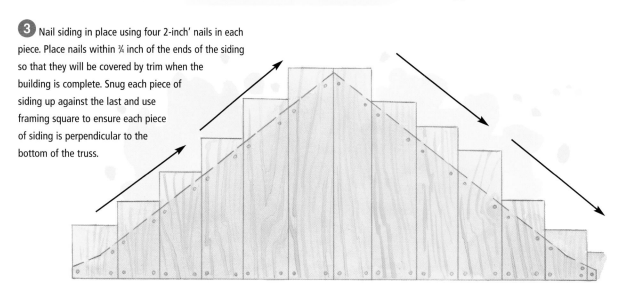

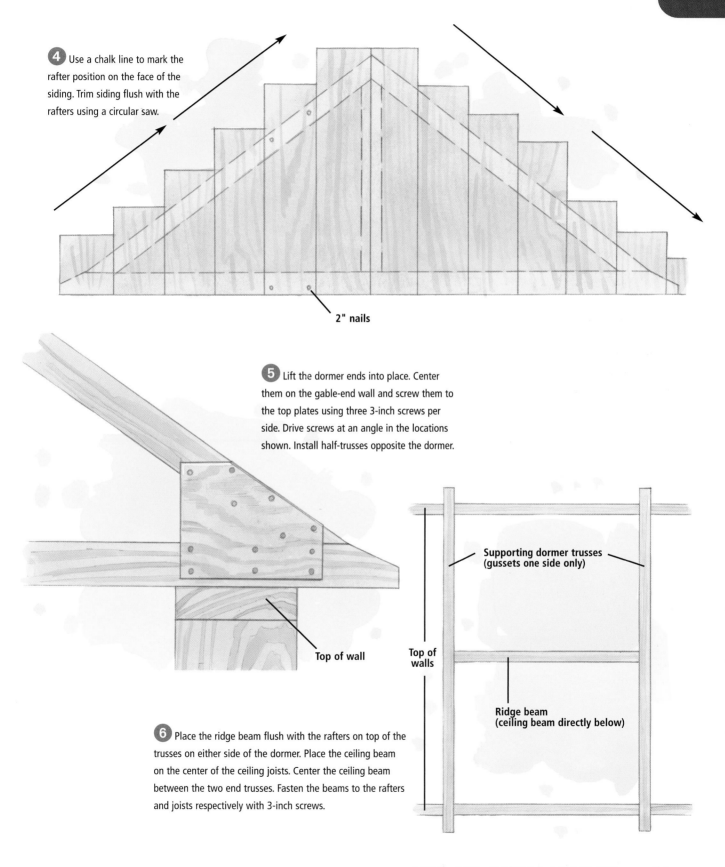

4 Use a chalk line to mark the rafter position on the face of the siding. Trim siding flush with the rafters using a circular saw.

2" nails

5 Lift the dormer ends into place. Center them on the gable-end wall and screw them to the top plates using three 3-inch screws per side. Drive screws at an angle in the locations shown. Install half-trusses opposite the dormer.

Top of wall

Supporting dormer trusses
(gussets one side only)

Top of walls

Ridge beam
(ceiling beam directly below)

6 Place the ridge beam flush with the rafters on top of the trusses on either side of the dormer. Place the ceiling beam on the center of the ceiling joists. Center the ceiling beam between the two end trusses. Fasten the beams to the rafters and joists respectively with 3-inch screws.

GABLE ROOF ASSEMBLY (continued)

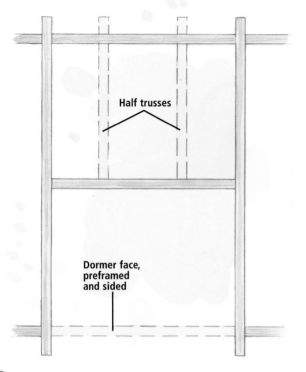

Half trusses

Dormer face, preframed and sided

7 Install half-trusses opposite the dormer face, spaced evenly between the full trusses. Screw through the beams and into the half-trusses with 3-inch screws.

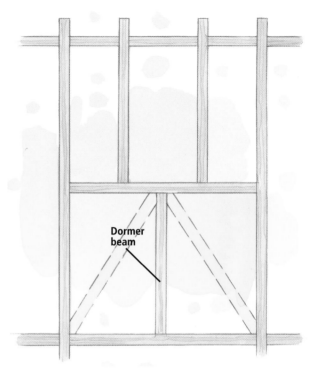

Dormer beam

8 Screw the dormer beam into the dormer peak so that it is flush with the peak. Level the beam with a carpenter's level, then fasten the dormer beam into the ridge beam with two 3-inch screws.

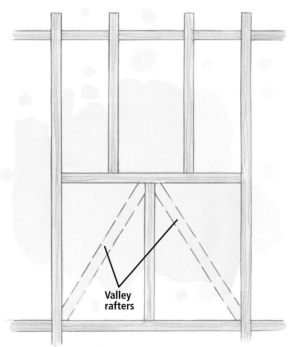

Valley rafters

9 Install valley rafters flush to the point where the truss and dormer face meet, using two 3-inch screws at top and bottom.

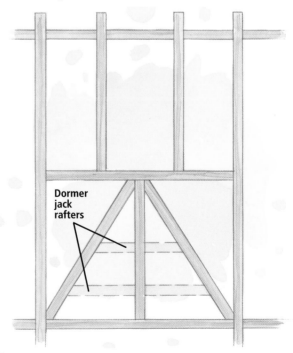

Dormer jack rafters

10 Install jack rafters between the dormer beam and the valley rafters. Screw into place with 3-inch screws.

11 Lift outside trusses into place so that the siding on the trusses is flush with the wall siding. Install screws at an angle at positions indicated by arrows.

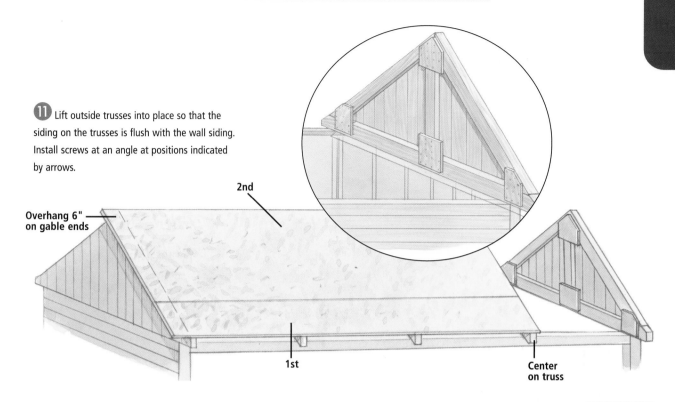

2nd

Overhang 6" on gable ends

1st

Center on truss

12 Place oriented-strand roof decking on the trusses, rough side up, in the order indicated on the drawing. Nail the decking to the trusses with 2-inch nails at 8-inch intervals, leaving a 6-inch overhang at each end of the building, and center the ends of the decking near the dormer over the trusses at each side of the dormer.

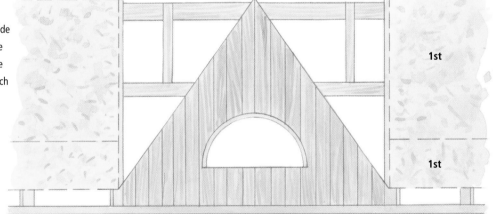

1st

1st

13 Cut decking pieces to fit around the dormer by measuring A and B, transferring the measurements to decking, and using a straightedge or chalk line to connect the marks for line C. Cut along the marks and nail the decking in place. Use the same method to cut decking for the dormer roof.

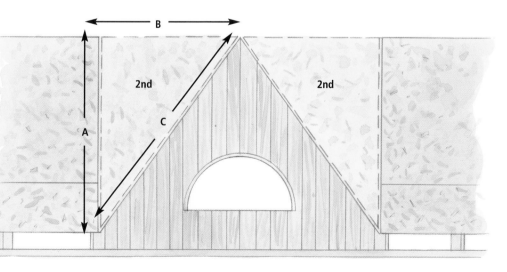

B

2nd

2nd

A

C

TRIM ASSEMBLY

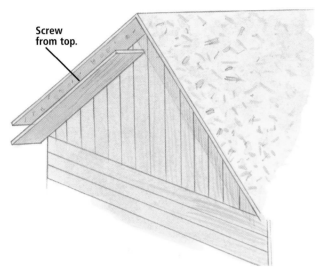

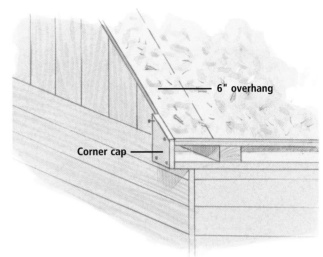

1 Install soffit trim on the underside of the roof decking on the gable ends of the building. Drive wood screws through the decking and into the soffit while holding the soffit tightly against the underside of the decking. Butt soffit board ends tightly against one another. Nail soffit trim on the underside of the trusses with two 2-inch nails per truss. Cut soffit so that joints are centered on the undersides of trusses; butt soffit trim ends tightly.

2 Nail corner caps to the soffit with four 2-inch nails.

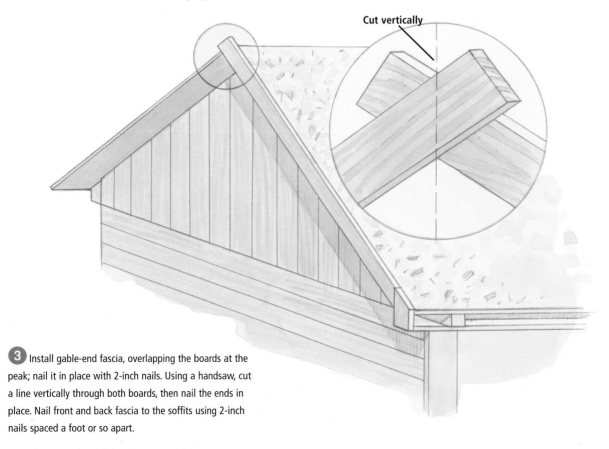

3 Install gable-end fascia, overlapping the boards at the peak; nail it in place with 2-inch nails. Using a handsaw, cut a line vertically through both boards, then nail the ends in place. Nail front and back fascia to the soffits using 2-inch nails spaced a foot or so apart.

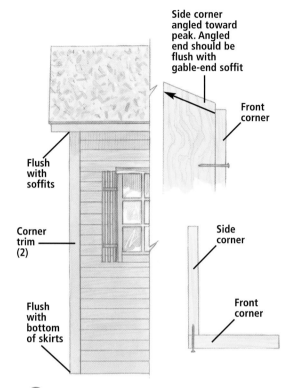

Side corner angled toward peak. Angled end should be flush with gable-end soffit

Front corner

Flush with soffits

Corner trim (2)

Side corner

Flush with bottom of skirts

Front corner

4 Install skirts around the base of the building, fastening them with 2-inch nails spaced a foot apart, flush with the bottom of the first course of siding. Nail corner trim to the front and back corners of the building, running the trim from the soffit to the bottom of the skirts. The front and back corner trim should overhang the siding on the gable end by the width of the trim board. Nail trim boards on the gable ends flush with the trim boards on the front and rear of the building.

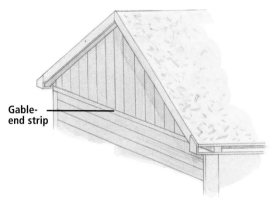

Gable-end strip

5 Install trim over the seam between the gable dormer and the gable wall, securing with 2-inch nails spaced about a foot apart.

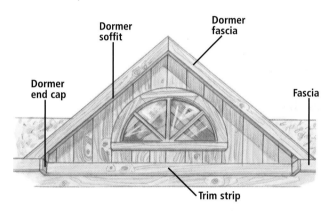

Dormer soffit

Dormer fascia

Dormer end cap

Fascia

Trim strip

6 Trim front dormer in the same manner as gable dormer. Install shutters, doors, and windows, shingle the roof, apply paint, and you're done!

BUILDING KIT

Buildings ordered in kit form have their components precision-cut from dried lumber in a factory. The parts are then labeled for easy assembly and packed for shipment, along with assembly directions. Putting them together is like assembling a puzzle. Unlike building from a plan, most, if not all, of the cutting, drilling, and shaping are done for you.

▶ **Neatly wrapped in plastic and mounted on a pallet, this building in kit form is as it will be delivered to its new owner.**

BUILDING A
GAZEBO

his 12-foot-wide hexagonal gazebo is big enough for family fun or parties. It's adaptable, too, as you can build it freestanding or attach it to a house or porch. You can screen it, if you like, for a bug-free retreat. A skylight unique to the design is charming, yet the gingerbread effect is easy to make. Because of its post foundation, size, and level of detail, this project is a bit more ambitious than the woodshed featured on pages 74–81. It requires a few more tools and somewhat more time and skill. If you're a moderately experienced do-it-yourselfer, you'll probably be able to finish the project in about three weekends.

Note: Unlike the other sheds and gazebos shown in this book, this gazebo is of a custom design and is not available in kit or plan form from an independent source. So we've provided a complete materials list, detailed dimension drawings, and step-by-step illustrated instructions that allow you to build it yourself.

Materials

Everything you need to build this gazebo is available from your local lumberyard or home center. The building uses standard dimension lumber, plywood, hardware, and roofing materials. (For more information on building materials, see pages 138–149)

MATERIALS

PART	NUMBER	MATERIAL	LENGTH	PART	NUMBER	MATERIAL	LENGTH
A1	6	4×4 PERIMETER POST	14'	Q	6	$^{11}\!/_{16} \times 2\frac{1}{4}$" COVE	6'11"
A2	1	4×4 CENTER POST	AS REQUIRED	R	1 ROLL	15-POUND FELT	
B	6	2×4 TOP PLATE	5'11½"	S		8" ALUMINUM FLASHING	45' TOTAL
C1	1	2×6 LONG DOUBLE JOIST	11'5"	T		METAL DRIP EDGE	41' TOTAL
C2	4	2×6 SHORT DOUBLE JOIST	5'7⅞"	U	2 SQUARES	CEDAR SHINGLES	
C3	6	2×6 JOIST BLOCKING	1'6"	V	6	1×6 SKYLIGHT BLOCKING	1'5"
C4	6	2×6 SHORT JOIST	3'6"	W	6	2×2 SKYLIGHT SPACER	1'6"
C5	6	2×8 BAND JOIST	5'8"	X	6	½" ACRYLIC PANEL	2' EACH SIDE
D	6	2×6 OUTER DECKING	5'9"	Y	6	⅜ ×1½" CEDAR CLEAT	1'9"
E	90	2×4 DECKING	309' TOTAL	Z	6	CEDAR RIDGE CAP	7'1"
F	1	2×12 DECK CENTER	SEE DRAWING	AA	8	RAILS	5'8"
G	6	2×12 ARCHED BEAM	5'8"	BB	44	1×6 NAIL SLATS	2'6"
H	1	KING POST	SEE DRAWING	CC	6	2×4 NAILER	5'7"
I	6	2×4 LONG ROOF RAFTER	7'3⅜"	DD	44	1×6 SIDE SLAT	1'7"
J	6	2×4 JOIST BLOCKING	1'7"	EE	4	STEP STRINGER	2'8"
K	6	2×4 SHORT JOIST	4'8"	FF	4	2×4 STEP NAILER	4'11"
L	6 SHEETS	¾" AC PLYWOOD		GG	4	1×8 STEP RISER	5'8"
M1	6	2×6 SOFFIT BLOCKING	SEE DRAWING	HH	2	1×6 RISER	5'2"
M2	6	2×8 SOFFIT SUPPORT	SEE DRAWING	II	16	2×4 STEP TREAD	5'6"
M3	6	2×2 SOFFIT NAILER	5'8"	JJ	6	8" STRAP HINGE	
N	6	1×8 SOFFIT	6'9"	KK	6	POST BASE	
O	6	1×6 FASCIA	6'10"	LL	6	DOUBLE JOIST HANGER	
P	6	¾ × ¾" SOFFIT COVE MOLDING	5'10"	MM	1	½" CARRIAGE BOLT	6"

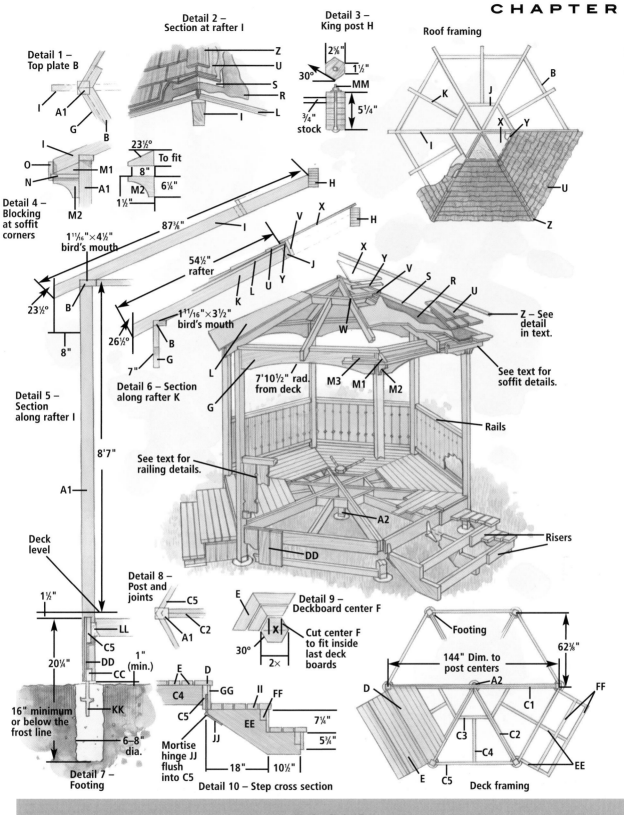

Detail 1 –
Top plate B

Detail 2 –
Section at rafter I

Detail 3 –
King post H

Roof framing

I
A1
G
B

Z
U
S
R
L
I

2⅝"
30°
1½"
MM
¾"
stock
5¼"

K
J
I
X
Y
I
U
Z
B

Detail 4 –
Blocking
at soffit
corners

I
O
N
M1
A1
M2
M2

23½°
To fit
8"
6¼"
1½"
M2

1¹¹⁄₁₆"×4½"
bird's mouth

87⅜"
I
H

54½"
rafter

V
X
J
Y
U
L
L
K

H

23½°
B
8"

26½°
B
G
7"

1¹¹⁄₁₆"×3½"
bird's mouth

Detail 6 – Section
along rafter K

X
Y
V
S
R
U

W
M3
M1
M2

Z – See
detail
in text.

See text for
soffit details.

Detail 5 –
Section
along rafter I

8'7"

A1

7'10½" rad.
from deck

L
G

Rails

See text for
railing details.

Deck
level

1½"

20¼"

16" minimum
or below the
frost line

A2

DD

Risers

LL
C5
DD
CC
KK
6–8"
dia.

1"
(min.)

Detail 7 –
Footing

Detail 8 –
Post and
joints

C5
C2
A1

Detail 9 –
Deckboard center F

E
x
30°
2×

Cut center F
to fit inside
last deck
boards

E
D
C4
C5
GG
JJ
II
FF
EE

7¼"
5¾"

18"
10½"

Mortise
hinge JJ
flush
into C5

Detail 10 – Step cross section

Footing

144" Dim. to
post centers

62⅜"

D
A2
C1
C3
C2
C4
E
C5
EE
FF

Deck framing

TOOLS

CIRCULAR SAW	MARKING PENCIL	SAFETY GOGGLES	8' STEPLADDER
PORTABLE TABLE SAW	FRAMING HAMMER	DUST MASK	SHOVEL
SABER SAW	CARPENTER'S LEVEL	WORK BOOTS	WHEELBARROW
DRILL-DRIVER	FRAMING SQUARE	WORK GLOVES	CEMENT
EXTENSION CORD	PLANE	CHALK LINE	
16' TAPE MEASURE	WOOD CHISEL	PLUMB BOB	

FOUNDATION

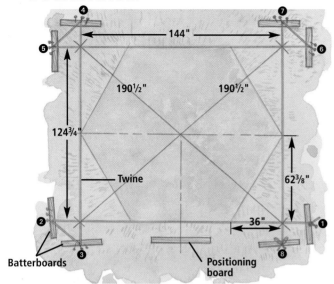

144"

190½"   190½"

124¾"

Twine

62⅜"

36"

Batterboards

Positioning board

POST FOUNDATIONS

Sinking posts into the ground and building atop them involves more work than on-ground methods, and is more permanent. It requires digging postholes and filling them with either poured concrete or a concrete footing topped by a wooden post in a mixture of crushed stone and sand. You'll probably want to rent a posthole digger and a cement mixer if you go this route. Advantages include:

■ **They're permanent.** If you're sure you won't need to move the building—and you want to make sure that no one else will—a post foundation ensures that what you build on it stays put.

■ **They're frost-proof.** If you're building where there are freeze-thaw cycles, burying posts in the ground that extend below the frost line means you're building is more likely to stay level than if it rests on top of the ground.

■ **They're low-impact.** Compared with pouring a concrete slab, a post foundation results in less site disturbance.

■ **They're inexpensive.** Fewer materials and less labor are required than are necessary for slab foundations

■ **They're relatively easy to build.**

1 Lay out the footings for the gazebo. Place a positioning board on edge in the approximate position you want the front of the gazebo. Pace out 8 feet from the center of the board on each side and erect a front set of batterboards at right angles to each other. Make batterboards from 3-foot 1×4s nailed to 2×2 stakes (see illustration, Step 2). Place two more sets 15 feet back from the front sets. Use 6d nails tacked into the tops of the boards for stringing and run stout twine from Point 1 parallel to your positioning board across to Point 2. Loop the twine around the nail at point 3, then to 4, 5, etc. until it gets to point 8 to form a rectangle. Now adjust the nail positions, using additional nails, along the board edges until the twine forms a 124¾×144-inch rectangle. This takes some practice, but you'll learn quickly.

2 Check the diagonals to be sure that each measures 190½ inches. Mark the intersection of the diagonals on the ground with crossed sticks or a stake. Then use the measurements in the drawing (above left) to mark the six footing points on the twine and directly below on the ground. Remove all nails in the boards, except the nails that define your final rectangle, then remove the twine. Dig 11-inch-diameter footing holes an inch deeper than your area frost line. Remember to dig the center hole.

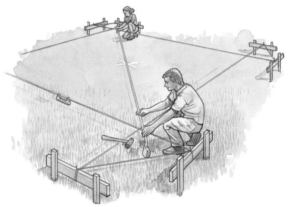

3 Position post bases by staking three 14-foot 2×4s across the holes. Restring the twine and measure again to mark exact position of bases on the 2×4s. Position and suspend the bases in the holes by tacking them to the 2×4s. Do not put a base in the center footing hole. Remove twine and batterboards. Fill holes with concrete. Remove 2×4s after two days.

STRUCTURE

1 Tack 4×4s into the post bases. Number each base and its 4×4 with a pencil. Start numbering at the tallest base. Then, using a level and chalk line, start at the top of this base and mark a level line on all the 4×4s. Take the 4×4s down, measure from the level line 10 feet 3¼ inches and cut the tops off the 4×4s. Replace and nail 4×4s into their respective post bases. Nail the 2×4 plates to the tops of the 4×4s. Position the joint of the plates over the 4×4 centerline.

2 Brace the 4×4s to keep them vertical and 11 feet 5 inches from the opposite post. Install the band joist. The top of the band joist is 8 feet 8½ inches from the plate top.

3 Install the 12-foot double floor joists in hanger brackets. Bend bracket flange to fit. Use 16d common nails.

4 Snap chalk lines across double-joist center from opposing 4×4 centers. Mark parallel lines on both sides of each chalk line. Transfer the marks down the joist side. Measure and cut other joists by these marks.

STRUCTURE (continued)

5 Cut double miters in four of the joists. To mark them, install the joists that take simple miters first, then measure and mark off the second cut that forms the double miter. Cut with a circular saw.

6 Tap the last joint in place with a hammer. It should be snug, but don't force it in so it bows. Nail it to its partner with 10d common nails. Now install the 2×6 blocking.

7 Nail the short joists in position between blocking and band joist. Place a piece of flashing on the center footing. Then wedge a section of 4×4 directly under the center of the double joist to rest on the flashing.

DECKING

1 Cut notches in outer decking piece to fit around the 4×4s. Nail it to the band joist. Then use a 16d nail as a spacing guide and begin adding the 2×4 decking. Line up your miters directly on the joist seams. Keep spacing uniform. Bore pilot holes for the nails.

2 Test-fit each ring of decking before you nail it down.

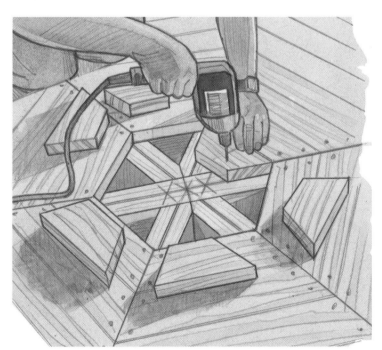

3 Bore pilot holes for nails in small deck pieces near the center. Do this even if the decking won't split while nailing. If any of these pieces are too snug, trim their edges slightly with a plane. If there's a gap, cut a new piece.

4 Place the center piece in position and nail. Cut it from a clear piece of 2×12.

ROOF STRUCTURE

1 Scribe the arch on the top beam with pencil and twine. The best way to do this is to tack a beam in position. Attach twine to a nail tacked into the center of outer decking piece. The arch runs off the beam 5 inches from the 4×4s. Take the beam down and cut the arch with a saber saw; then use this piece as a template to mark the other beam pieces.

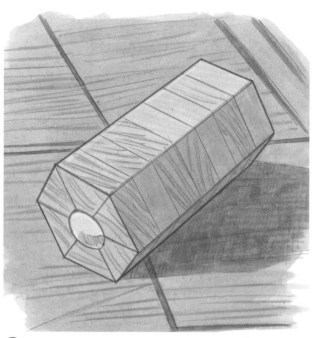

2 Make the roof's king post from laminated sections of 1×4. Use glue and a zinc-plated 6 inch-long ½-inch carriage bolt, nut, and washer.

3 Toenail the long rafters into the king post to begin roof construction. Then install rafter blocking around the king post.

4 Install the short rafters with 16d common nails.

ROOF

1 Attach the plywood roof sections with some help. Then cover the roof with 15-pound roofing felt.

2 Begin soffit construction with the triangular blocking under the long rafter ends. Then attach the 2×2 soffit nailer that abuts the 4×4s.

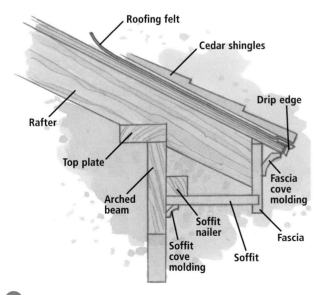

Roofing felt

Cedar shingles

Drip edge

Rafter

Top plate

Arched beam

Fascia cove molding

Soffit nailer

Soffit cove molding

Fascia

Soffit

3 This profile drawing shows the soffit at the arched beam, plate, and short rafter. Attach the cove molding after you attach the corner supports butting it against the supports. Add the metal roof edge around the edge of the plywood. To prepare for the cedar shingles, nail flashing over the joints on the roof.

4 Begin shingle work with a double layer of shingles at the bottom of each roof section.

ROOF (continued)

5 Cut angled shingles for the joints with a portable tablesaw. The shingles are too small to hold while cutting with a circular saw or handsaw.

6 Tack a straightedge to the first row of shingles 5 inches above the edge. Then abut the second row of shingles against this guide. Repeat this step as you work your way up.

SKYLIGHT

1 Cut acrylic sections for the skylight with a saber saw. Acrylic sheets come with a protective plastic film on both sides. Leave this film on until you are ready to screw the sections down.

2 Apply a bead of clear silicone caulk to the skylight blocking. Apply it also to the spacers as you work your way around the skylight. Then caulk between the panels.

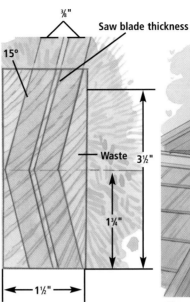

3 Drill two ⅛-inch-diameter shank holes in each acrylic panel side. Then bore pilot holes into the wood. Use countersunk 1½-inch No. 6 screws for panels, then attach cedar cleats.

4 Cut roof caps from a cedar 2×4 with a portable tablesaw. This drawing shows you how to cut two caps from one length of 2×4. Set the blade at 15 degrees, make top and bottom cuts, and then just move the fence.

5 Attach the cedar cap that fits over the roof and the acrylic panel joints. Miter the tops and use galvanized finishing nails.

RAILING

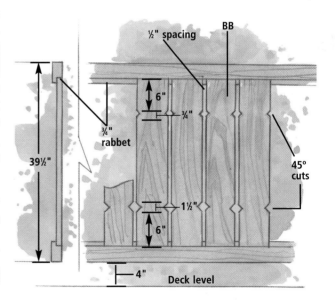

1 Attach the side slats with 7d galvanized common nails. Don't attach to stair sides.

2 Use this drawing to measure and mark the slatted side panels. The decorative rows of diamonds are formed by large and small V-cuts in each slat.

RAILING *(continued)*

3 Make the cuts that form the diamonds. Square up and clamp a stack of slats together. Put the clamps on the ends so they won't interfere with cutting. Set your circular saw blade at 45 degrees. Make the cuts from one side of the stack, then turn the stack around and repeat.

4 Nail the slats to the rails with 1¼-inch galvanized wood shingle nails. Use ½-inch spacers. Keep it all square.

5 Install the panels with 6d nails. Remember not to nail panels on the sides where steps will be installed.

STAIRS

1 Chisel out mortises in the band joists for the stair's three 8-inch strap hinges. There's no need to mortise the hinges on the stringers. These hinges allow the stairs to move with frost heaves.

2 Nail the 2×4 treads down with 10d common nails after you attach the side slats. Use a 16d nail as a spacer.

Congratulations! Prime with an oil-base primer and apply two coats of latex outdoor paint. Coat floor and steps with clear varnish.

BUILDING A
POTTING SHED

▲ **This panelized "sun shed" is buildable in a few hours. It takes advantage of a southern exposure, a raised bed on the sunny side, and lots of heat-soaking flagstone to create a warm microclimate that flowers love.**

Here's a potting shed that combines the functions of a storage shed, potting shed, and greenhouse in one easy-to-assemble structure. Its saltbox design starts with a back wall that's free of windows and doors for maximum hanging space, then adds a 12/12 pitch glazed roof that's designed to be oriented south for maximum light and solar heat gain. The design offers a light, airy interior that's pleasant to work in. Add a potting bench, and you have an ideal location to give seedlings a jump on the growing season.

This building is delivered to your site as a panelized kit. The walls, roof, and floor of a panelized building are constructed in factory. All you need to do is create a foundation,

screw or bolt the panels together, install doors and windows, and finish the building with paint or stain. Depending on their size, complexity, and design, panelized buildings can be erected in a very short time—sometimes as little as a few hours to a weekend. Often, preparing the site and building the foundation takes more time than does assembling the structure. A wide variety of sheds and gazebos

MATERIALS	
BUILDING KIT	
6	4×8×16-INCH SOLID CONCRETE BLOCKS
4	6×6 TREATED LANDSCAPE TIMBERS
5	TIMBER SPIKES OR LAG BOLTS

are available in panelized kits from a number of building manufacturers.

Panelized buildings even have an advantage over ready-built structures: Because two people can carry the panels, the buildings can be erected in locations that are inaccessible to delivery trucks and trailers. If you're interested in siting an outbuilding in a courtyard, a fenced backyard, or down a winding woodland path, panelized structures can be placed there– without requiring the assembly time of a building constructed from plans or precut lumber. Also, panelized buildings can be taken apart and reassembled elsewhere, so you can take them with you if you move.

Materials

This shed features stud-wall construction and is sheathed with T-111 plywood siding for a classic, barnlike look. The roof is covered with conventional three-tab asphalt shingles. Roof glazing is a special composite that combines the antiyellowing properties of acrylic with the shatter resistance of polycarbonate. A two-part Dutch door allows opening just the top portion for ventilation or additional light. The shed's owner can insulate it with conventional fiberglass insulation batts or rigid foam panels for year-round use.

TOOLS

CARPENTER'S LEVEL

TAPE MEASURE

SOCKET WRENCH

SCREWDRIVER

HAMMER

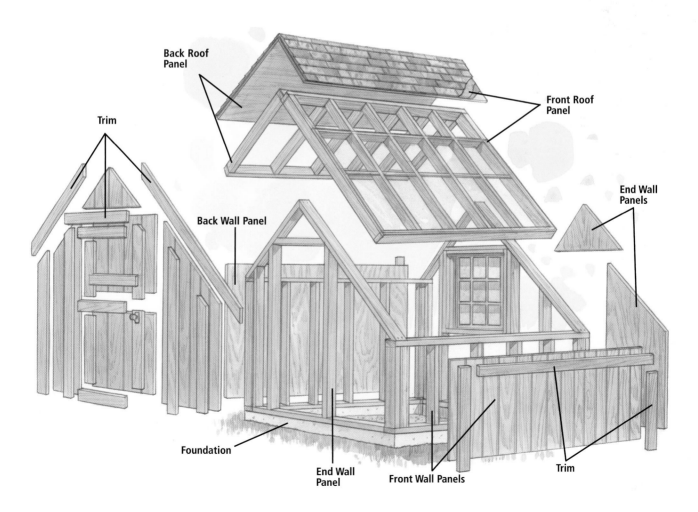

Back Roof Panel

Front Roof Panel

Trim

Back Wall Panel

End Wall Panels

Foundation

End Wall Panel

Front Wall Panels

Trim

BUILDING THE FOUNDATION

This kit can be ordered with or without a plywood floor and accepts two kinds of foundations.

Option one is a gravel floor. It's a good choice for areas with less-than-perfect drainage or if you're going to use the building as a greenhouse and want runoff from plant watering to drain directly through a gravel floor into the ground. In that case, clear brush or remove sod and level the site. Dig a bed larger than the building by 1 foot on all sides to allow water running off the roof to drain properly. Fill the bed with 4 inches of gravel and lay treated landscape timbers on the gravel. Level the timbers with a carpenter's level. Spike or lag the timbers together; square by measuring the diagonals and adjust timbers until the measurements are the same.

Option two is a concrete block foundation. Position six 4×8×16-inch solid concrete blocks in the form of a rectangle the same dimensions of the building. Square the blocks by measuring diagonals as above. Then, using a flat-bladed spade, cut into the sod around each block. Move the block and remove the sod within the incisions. Replace the blocks and level them by adding or removing soil beneath each block until it is level in both directions. Lay the landscape timber frame on the blocks, checking for square. Level the frame using blocks, boards, and/or asphalt shingle shims between the blocks resting on the ground and the landscape timbers.

BLOCK FOUNDATIONS

Concrete blocks vie with wood skids (which can either rest on blocks or directly on the ground) in the easy-to-build foundation department. With the block method, solid concrete blocks rest on the ground, and the building's floor stringers rest on the blocks. Block foundations are a bit more trouble to build than skid foundations, as the blocks have to be absolutely level and evenly spaced. And you can't tow the building around your yard after it's constructed as you can a building on skids. That said, block foundations have some significant advantages:

◀ **You can cope with a slope.** Skid foundations are generally limited to fairly level ground. But you can stack blocks to cope with moderate grade changes, making blocks the foundation of choice if you have an uneven building site. If your ground is very uneven, you can use precast pier blocks. These allow you to rest the edge of a joist in a slot cast in the top of the block where the ground is relatively level. Where the ground drops away from the building's floor, you can cut a 4×4 post and place it securely in a square, recessed hole in the top of the block, allowing you to level the building more precisely and less expensively than by simply stacking solid blocks under that part of the building.

▶ **You can build a larger building.** Skid-founded buildings are limited by the length of the timbers used for the skids. Using a block foundation means you can build a larger building—and you don't have to transport long, heavy, preservative-soaked timbers to your building site. Blocks are heavy, to be sure, but much more compact and easier to handle than timbers.

ERECT THE WALL PANELS

The panels are pre-drilled for fast and accurate assembly. Simply have a helper hold each panel in place while you lag-bolt the panels snug to the floor and to each other. The door and gable window are already installed.

LIFT THE ROOF INTO PLACE

The roof is the heaviest panel and is best handled by three people. First, lift the top edge of the roof onto the top plates of the wall panels. Then slide the roof into place and lag-bolt it snug.

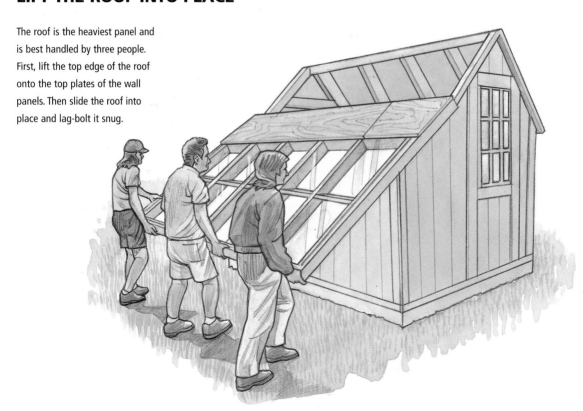

▲ Inside, there's plenty of room for potting,
puttering, and storing garden tools and supplies.

■ Nestled into the back of this lot on an old New England estate, this new storage shed is sited to provide a convenient spot for garden tools and lawn equipment.

BUILDING BASICS

Now that you've decided what kind of outbuilding you want, it's time to determine exactly where you want to put your building. This chapter will walk you through the siting process. You'll start by making a base map of your property that shows its existing features, plus any setbacks, easements, or utility lines that may restrict where you can build. (You'll also discover ways to gain more flexibility than codes may appear to allow.)

Next, you'll learn how to perform a step-by-step analysis of your lot, inventorying those features you want

to make the most of and noting those features you'd like to improve. You'll consider how the project you're thinking of may help you to not only gain a building but improve your whole outdoor living space. You'll also learn how to determine what size outbuilding you'll need.

Once you've surveyed your lot for possible sites and determined exactly what the dimensions of your building should be, it's time to draw up a master plan of your project. This chapter will show you how. Finally, you'll learn how to prepare the site.

MAKING A BASE MAP

Start your planning with a base map—an overhead diagram of your property that includes property lines and major features, such as the house, outbuildings, and trees. The easiest way to develop a base map is to make a scaled copy of your plat or other official map. You might find such a map among the papers from the closing of the purchase of your home or from your county tax assessor. In many communities, the tax assessor has a website from which you can download a map of your lot.

▼ Use graph paper to draw your property's features to scale.

What the base map should show

■ The distance of major elements, such as trees, the house, or a detached garage, from the property lines and from each other.

■ Location of doors and windows and what rooms they are in.

■ The overhang of roof eaves beyond the walls of the house (if you are building a new deck or patio as part of the project).

■ Downspouts and runoff direction.

■ Topography—the direction and pitch of slopes or major changes in the ground level.

Marking your restrictions

Next, call your planning and zoning department and utility company and ask them what, if any, restrictions apply to the project you're thinking of. Draw these restrictions on your base map as well.

IN THE ZONE

Sometimes zoning regulations go beyond simply specifying "no build" zones such as those outlined on page 119. The following four basic building regulations can't be drawn on your map, but be aware of them before you build:

■ Height rules specify the maximum height of a building.

■ Width rules denote the maximum allowable width and depth of the building.

■ Use rules specify its allowable uses, which include residential, commercial, industrial, and home-office considerations.

■ Density specifies the number of building units allowed per acre.

Meet at least briefly with your local building code officials to see if you need a building permit to do what you're planning and to make sure your project won't violate any zoning restrictions.

Planning and zoning restrictions might include the following:

■ **Setbacks.** Setback requirements mandate the number of feet between the building area and the property line. The best way to check your setback restrictions is to review your lot's survey plat. If you do not have a copy, request one from your local municipality authority. To protect yourself from costly changes, do not build a permanently placed outbuilding outside of your property's approved buildable area.

■ **Easements.** An easement is a legal interest in a parcel of land that is owned by someone other than the landowner. The homeowner does not own the rights to the land use on an easement, even though it is on his or her property. For example, utility companies most likely have easements on your lot so that they can run sewer or power lines on your property. You are not allowed to place any permanent structures on most easement areas. In some instances, outbuildings or fences are allowed.

Utility lines

Call your local utility companies—gas, electricity, water, and telephone—to have them mark underground utility lines on your property. It is crucial to know where these lines are, even if you are excavating only a few inches. Depths of the lines can vary. Many states offer a one-call service for utility marking; call the North American One Call Referral System at 888/258-0808. Ask to have the route and depth of each utility line marked. Also find and mark all sprinkler lines and outdoor lighting wires, if you have those.

PERMANENT VERSUS NONPERMANENT

Note that most restrictions apply to "permanent" buildings. If you find out that codes and restrictions hem in your placement options, you may be able to gain flexibility by making your project portable. A shed on skids, for example, or one that simply rests on a gravel foundation (see "Foundation, Foundation, Foundation" pages 40–41) can be moved easily, so the restrictions that apply to permanent structures may not apply to them. Check with your local code officials.

▲ **Armed with colored pencils and a garden template, embellish a bird's-eye-view drawing of your property with the components of your landscape. Then add the footprint of your proposed outbuilding, along with any other landscaping additions, such as fences, paths, or plants.**

▲ **If you're planning on making a number of landscaping changes when you build your outbuilding, you may want to hire a landscape designer to come up with a comprehensive plan for your yard.**

ANALYZING THE SITE

Aesthetic concerns

Before you look for a specific spot on which to build your project, consider your lot as a whole. Consider these steps no matter what kind of an outbuilding you're planning. Draw the results of your analysis on the base map as you go.

■ **Build on the north of the lot.** In a study in a Berkeley, California, neighborhood, residents were shown a plan of their lot and were asked to circle the areas in their yard in which they spent the most time. In nearly every case, they circled areas with a southern exposure. Like plants, people are drawn to sunlight. Make the most of your yard by building your outbuilding on its northern edge, leaving the sunny southern stretch for outdoor living. Placing an outbuilding on a lot's northern edge with its long dimension on an east-west axis has an additional benefit: A blank south-facing wall will reflect sunlight back into the yard, creating a warm, bright microclimate that both plants and people will love. If you're planning a greenhouse, building on the north edge of your lot allows you to control what's to the south of the greenhouse. Building a greenhouse against the south edge of your property, however, puts its sun exposure at the mercy of your neighbor to the south, who may decide to plant trees, build a fence, or construct an outbuilding that could shade your project.

■ **Inventory the lot's best features.** Walk your lot carefully at various times of the day to get a sense of what you like best about it and *don't* want to disturb with your outbuilding project. Tie bright orange ribbon around trees and plants you want to preserve. If some exceptional plants or small trees are growing in what will become excavated ground for a foundation, or are the route of a new path or patio created by your project, consider marking them with a different-color ribbon for transplanting.

■ **Note your lot's worst features.** All parts of a lot are often not in equally good condition. Perhaps a wind or ice storm has mangled a grove of trees. Perhaps a corner of the land was

▶ Building this screen house was the first step in reclaiming the least attractive part of this otherwise pleasant wooded lot. Formerly a rubble-strewn hillside, this corner of the yard nonetheless had a fine view of the main house. The screen house capitalizes on that vista and offers a focal point for the view from the home's windows. Building it inspired the owners to start landscaping the area with lawns, flower beds, and paths—work still in progress.

used as a refuse dump, or the land was scarred by a previous owner's misuse. Perhaps a concrete slab from an old garage is present. Consider redeeming such places by siting your outbuilding there. That way, you displace the damage, avoid disrupting your lot's best features, and don't have to repair the damage. And, using an existing slab in good condition for a foundation can save you a great deal of trouble and expense.

■ **Orient the building to the sun and wind.** People have the same preference for sunny interior spaces that they do for sunny yards. If you're building a storage shed, this may not matter, but if you're going to be spending substantial time in your outbuilding,

you'll be much happier in a sunny space. So, if possible, stretch out the building along an east-west axis, and locate the places you'll spend most time in on the south side. That's where you'll want your potting bench, workbench, or seating area. If you have a garden and a great southern exposure, consider building a dual-purpose structure, with a greenhouse as one of its functions. You also might want to use your outbuilding to shelter a portion of your yard—a patio or garden, for instance—from cold fall and winter winds. Conversely, you might be able to use a building's long face to catch and funnel cooling summer breezes to the same areas during the hot season.

▶ Thanks to clever siting, this shed serves three purposes: Its sitting porch offers a great water view; the structure adds a cabin-on-a-lake appeal to the small pond; and the space inside is used to store fishing and canoeing gear.

BUBBLE AND MASTER PLANS

A bubble plan shows how you use different areas in your yard. A master plan shows all the elements in the landscape design, both the hardscape and the planting beds. Both plans are handy if you are building a structure as part of a landscape makeover. If you are simply adding a shed or gazebo to an existing plan, skip these plans and make scale drawings of the project itself.

To make a bubble plan, tape tracing paper over your base map. Mark different areas of the yard by drawing circles or ovals, then label how each one is used. Tape another piece of tracing paper over the base map to make a master plan. Draw all the landscape details on the plan.

■ **Create outdoor rooms.** When siting your outbuilding, consider the shapes it will leave on your lot. People feel most comfortable when some feeling of containment exists and prefer courtyards, for example, to wide-open spaces. Make the most of this preference for coziness by placing your building so that it works with your house, garage, and any walls, fences, or other yard features to give shape to the spaces that surround and furnish and equip your space for the kinds of uses you enjoy most: gardening, relaxing, entertaining, sports, or family projects and activities. To make these "rooms" even more attractive, you can reduce noise and increase privacy by placing either your outbuilding or a sturdy fence between your yard and a busy street, for example.

■ **Consider noise.** A strategically placed shed can block traffic noise, creating an oasis of relative quiet in your yard. Conversely, you'll want to place a gazebo away from excessive background noise so you can enjoy relaxed conversation with family and guests.

■ **Consider the view.** Note the best vistas on your lot and consider how you might place your outbuilding so as not to block these vistas from your house. Also consider how you might use your outbuilding to your advantage to block a less-than-picturesque aspect of your neighbor's house or yard.

▼ **This series of three interconnected gazebos serve as outdoor dining and entertaining rooms for large groups. They also add a pleasing sense of enclosure to the lawn.**

HIGH-TECH PLANNING

If you're planning to redesign you landscape, consider using landscape-design software to simplify the job. The programs are easy to use and flexible and can speed your progress from base plan to final design. You'll find them especially useful when making changes—you can alter your plans without having to redraw them.

The programs calculate dimensions of each structure, create side elevations and three-dimensional views, make materials lists, and create repeating patterns on walkways. You can even place trees and shrubs where you want them.

Home improvement and gardening magazines often review the newest programs which you can buy from computer stores. Or check out local home improvement or building supply centers—many offer computer design services without cost if you purchase your materials from them.

Sizing Up your Project

Paint the ground

No matter what kind of structure you plan to buy or build, outline its rough dimensions on the yard with spray paint. This ground-marking paint was developed primarily for road maintenance purposes. Unlike ordinary household spray paint, which won't work if inverted, this paint is designed to spray when the can is held nozzle-side down, making it an excellent way to mark the perimeter of your project. If you prefer, you can mark the site with lime or flour instead.

Erect story poles

For an even more complete visual sense of the space the building will occupy, use story poles. These simple wood poles (2×2s with a sharpened end simply pounded into the ground) work well for relatively small, one-story structures. Use poles at least 2 feet longer than your building will be high so you can sink them into the ground deep enough for them to stand securely. Cut off any excess height once you've implanted them. Now you have a three-dimensional outline of the building's mass and can get a better idea of how it will affect your property's views and sense of enclosure.

▼ The owner of this small storage shed assembled all the gear he wanted to store in order to determine the size shed he needed. You may find, as this owner did, that you don't need as large a shed as you first supposed.

Evaluate the size

Once you've painted the building's perimeter on the ground, fill it up with your building's intended contents, be it equipment, plants, or people, to see if the size building you're considering is large enough to serve its intended purpose.

If you're building a storage shed, will all your current or planned equipment fit in comfortably? Does the design leave space for you to walk in all the way to the back wall and wheel out every piece of equipment, or will you have to crawl over things to get to the tool you want and deal with gridlock every time you want to pull the garden tractor out?

If you're planning a potting shed, mark out the location of a potting bench, storage shelves, or any other interior amenities to get a sense of the space.

If a workshop is in your plans, wheel your workbench and equipment to the site. Make sure that it will fit, and that there's the necessary clearance required to, for example, rip a full sheet of plywood on your tablesaw or perform any other operation your work might require.

If you plan on a screen house or gazebo, set your patio furniture inside the sprayed outline. Imagine the floor space as it will be when finally furnished. Does everything seem to fit? Envision the space with family and guests. Can people move around easily inside or will they be reduced to elbow room only?

▲ **This gazebo is plenty large for a crowd. A large circular table and set of chairs convert it to a spacious dining pavilion.**

CLEARING AND LEVELING

Clear the project area of all weeds, including a space of several feet around the project. Remove all perennial weeds and their roots, particularly in excavations of less than 4 inches. You can either spray the area with a glyphosate-based weed killer a week before starting the project, or simply clear away the weeds by slicing off and removing the top 2 inches of soil. Do this by digging with a square-nose shovel held nearly horizontally. If only a few weeds exist, water the area, then pull them by hand.

■ **Cut down trees in the way.** Call a professional tree service to deal with large trees, as attempting to remove them yourself

can be dangerous. You'll also need to remove the stump and major roots during excavation for any tree that was growing in the project area if installing a slab foundation, mortared pathway, patio, or wall.

The amount of time you spend clearing the project area of vegetation depends on the nature of the project and what's growing there–another reason to choose your project site carefully.

Consider grading and drainage

You must consider drainage anytime the landscape is altered. An outbuilding installed in a low-lying area where the soil contains clay or otherwise does not drain well may be prone to flooding. Installing perforated drainpipe is one solution for potential drainage problems in poorly draining soils.

If your soil drains normally and the foundation is generally on the same grade as its surroundings, you should not encounter problems with excess moisture.

Where an outbuilding is sited against or near the house, grade at least one-third of the ground next to the new outbuilding so it gradually slopes down and away from the house and outbuilding. Build the outbuilding foundation at or above the existing grade surrounding the house. Complete the grading of the area before you lay out and excavate your project.

◀ **The site of this newly built maple-sugaring shed was carefully cleared and leveled before the shed was constructed. Landscaping will be the final step in completing the project.**

CHOOSING A BUILDING

Your land is mapped, your site is chosen and prepared. Now it's time to choose the building itself. In this chapter, you'll encounter some of the considerations you want to keep in mind. These include: finding a building with a style that complements, if not matches, your home, and the various key elements that compose an architectural style; how to choose a plan, including tips on how to visualize a building using study plans, renderings, and photographs; and how to choose a source, be it a plan publisher or building manufacturer, including a detailed description of what to look for in various types of plan and building packages. You'll learn about shipping costs and access concerns, which will prepare you to have a lumber package, panelized building package, or complete building shipped to your site. Finally, you'll read about foundation types, as these may affect what building you choose and how you choose to construct it.

▶ **This handsome and functional combination potting and storage shed adds its dignified presence to a formal urban garden.**

CHOOSING A STYLE

◀ **The combination of octagonal structural geometry and cedar shingles turns the ceiling of this gazebo into a pleasing abstract composition.**

No matter what purpose your outbuilding will have, it will be a significant addition to your property–perhaps even a focal point to your yard. So you'll want to make sure that the building's design complements your home.

Fortunately, you can choose from literally thousands of outbuilding designs. The manufacturers and plan publishers that appear in this book's "Resources" section, beginning on page 168, are a great place to start looking. Peruse their websites or order their catalogs, and you'll find buildings designed to complement just about any home style, from colonial to contemporary and everything in between. Some manufacturers specialize in a certain regional or period style; others produce buildings in a variety of styles. And if you don't find a building that suits your preferences from among these companies' stock designs, just ask. Many will customize their designs–or design a new building from scratch to your specifications.

Here are some guidelines to help you narrow down your choices when looking:

■ **Materials.** Your building's materials should complement those on your house whenever possible. Pay particular attention to roofing and sheathing options, as walls and roofs are the most visible part of the building. Fortunately, the diminutive size of most outbuildings allows you to splurge a bit on these materials and still stay within budget. If your house has a shake roof and unpainted cedar lap siding, you can duplicate this treatment on a potting shed without breaking the bank.

■ **Colors.** If your outbuilding is paintable, you can create design harmony in several ways: by duplicating your home's color scheme, by painting the outbuilding the color of your home's trim, or by painting it a color that complements an aspect of its environment. Gardeners often take particular pleasure in coordinating their outbuilding's color scheme with that of the surrounding landscaping.

■ **Rooflines.** Especially if your outbuilding is near the house, a similar roof slope will lend an eye-pleasing congruence to the scene.

■ **Details.** Your choice of windows, doors, shutters, porches, and ornament all offer opportunities to match or complement those on your residence.

◀ A farmhouse and its front-yard playhouse take architectural harmony to a fanciful extreme: The outbuilding is a scaled-down version of the main house, a folly that causes passing motorists to do a quick double take.

■ **Use.** It's possible to design a storage shed that looks like a pool house or a potting shed that looks like a playhouse, and such a cross-dressed design could serve as an amusing folly. But there's something inherently attractive about a building that honestly proclaims its function—especially when that function, such as that of a greenhouse or potting shed, is a natural part of the landscape.

■ **To thine own self be true.** Keep in mind that the outbuilding must be true to its own style. Putting a Victorian color scheme and ornament on a contemporary outbuilding will just result in an amateurish, muddled look. And nothing requires your outbuilding to match your house exactly. Just as several different architectural styles can coexist in a neighborhood, so can a home and its outbuilding have a somewhat different look. Just ensure that the two buildings do not represent completely different aesthetics.

▶ A two-colored paint scheme adds punch to this cute and classic storage shed.

CHOOSING A PLAN

The ideal way to choose a building, of course, is to see it in person, walk around and inside it, and visualize how you'll use it, where you'll site it, and how you'll arrange its interior design and contents. Such a personal inspection also can let you examine the quality of the materials, and, if you're buying a completed building or panelized package, the quality of the manufacturer's product.

That's not always possible, especially if you're ordering a building from a distant source. You can, however, ask the building manufacturer or plan publisher if it knows of a similar building that's been constructed in your area, and if so whether you can contact that building's owner. It might well be worth a trip, not only to have a look at the building in person, but to talk to the owner about his or her experience in dealing with the manufacturer and with the quality of the building, its materials, plans, and instructions.

Failing that, you'll have to make a decision based on a two-dimensional representation of your building—a study plan, an illustrated rendering, or photographs. Each has its advantages and disadvantages:

A study plan is a rudimentary plan of the building sometimes offered to potential customers at no cost so that they may study the design to decide whether they wish to purchase the full set of plans. Generally, study plans include a plan view, which offers a bird's-eye view of the building's floor plan, and one or more elevations, which view the building straight on from a side. Elevations may show any side of the building. Exterior elevations will show exterior features and details, as though you're standing outside the building looking at one wall; interior elevations look at the wall from the inside. Study plans are extremely useful for getting an exact idea of the dimensions of the building and any interior spaces and for specifying materials and details.

◄ This glazed-roof potting shed has a simple design that's easy to understand from this promotional photo.

◀ Some product websites, catalogs, and brochures also feature interior shots. These can be helpful, but keep in mind that photos taken with a wide-angle lens can make interiors appear much larger than they actually are.

However, some laypeople find it a bit difficult to visualize a building from the study plan's separate, two-dimensional views.

A rendering is designed to give those unused to reading plans an illustration of what the completed building might look like. It may be from an oblique point of view that allows you to see more than one side. It might offer a cutaway perspective so that you can see both the outside and the inside in one glance. Like study plans, renderings may show both interior and exterior views. Although they can be useful, view them with some caution: Remember, these are idealized artists' illustrations designed to show the building in its most pleasing light. A rendering may—and often does—show the building in an attractive, landscaped setting, with colors and light that would make almost any building look good. When looking at a rendering, make sure you're attracted to the building itself and not just the image on the paper. Also, find out if the rendering includes options and upgrades such as additional windows or upgraded siding material that aren't

included in the building's base price. Be aware that it is possible for a building to look great in a rendering but function terribly in the real world if, for example, windows are not placed at eye level or a picturesquely steep roof slope cuts dramatically into precious storage space.

Photographs would seem to be the gold standard, as you're seeing the real thing. They also can be very helpful, especially if you have access to photographs from many perspectives and if detail shots of features and materials are included. As with a rendering, try to separate your response to the building from your response to its setting. And be aware that clever camera positions and wide-angle lenses can make buildings look larger than they really are.

While your best judgment will probably result from seeing the building in person, a combination of study plans, renderings, and/or photographs can get you pretty close. Just make sure you pay as much attention to hard facts such as dimensions and material specifications as you do to attractive pictures.

Choosing a Source

▲ A craftsman installs the roof on this shed, which was purchased as a completed building. Materials were hand-carried to the site, then erected on a concrete block foundation.

Outbuildings are available from sources ranging from mom-and-pop operations that build a few sheds a year as a sideline to large manufacturers that sell hundreds of different buildings over the Web and/or through national distributors. No particular type of source is necessarily better than another, and your first step will probably be to look for a building of the style and type you like, then narrow down the field to a few favorites.

Once you've found some buildings with a look you like and the dimensions, configuration, and features you need, it's time to read the fine print. First, you'll want to determine exactly what you're getting. Then you'll want to figure your total costs for the building, including shipping and set-up, if applicable. Once you've determined those factors, you'll be in a better position to choose a building and supplier.

CHOOSING A PRODUCT TYPE

Many manufacturers make buildings available in several forms: as plans and instructions, as a precut lumber package, as a panelized package, or as a ready-built structure. Here's what should be included in each type:

Plans and instructions

The quality and detail of building plans can vary widely. Unless the building is a very simple one and you're a proficient carpenter, you'll probably want not only highly detailed building plans, but instructions as well.

Before you buy, ask what comes with the package. (Some manufacturers make plans downloadable from their website, or include typical examples in their catalog.) Look for the following:

■ **A detailed materials list with quantities, grades, and types of materials specified exactly.** This list should be so complete that you can take it to a lumberyard or home center, hand it to the clerk at the building supplies order desk, and leave with everything you need. The list should include not only the lumber and major components of the building but all the hardware, fasteners, and other materials it will require. The list should also include enough overage in quantity to account for waste and the occasional mistake on the part of the builder. (For more information on materials, see pages 138–149.)

■ **A list of the tools required to complete the project, from pencil and ruler to power tools.** This list will let you know if you need to purchase or rent tools to complete the

job—and will allow you to include such expenditures in your budget for the project. (For more information on tools, see pages 152–161.)

■ **Foundation specifications.** Plans generally don't include directions for building a foundation, but they should clearly state what kind of foundation is required, along with its dimensions and other specifications. (For more information on foundation types, see pages 40–41.)

■ **Illustrated, step-by-step instructions.** Even for a small building, these instructions can run to a dozen pages or more. Ideally, they'll include numbered or clearly delineated steps, accompanied by detailed, annotated drawings, schematics, illustrations, or photographs showing each completed step, and illustrating how to perform any unfamiliar techniques required.

Instructions should be clearly written and easy to understand, with any specialized terminology defined either in an accompanying glossary or in the text of the instructions itself.

Notes to the builder, sidebars, or introductions to each section should give you a sense of the flow of the work, of what each step accomplishes, and why they are ordered as they are. The better you understand the overall process, the easier it will be for you to follow the individual steps. Instructions should also indicate when a helper is required to perform a step safely.

Finally, instructions should be printed in reasonably sized type with plenty of white space around them. This may seem trivial—until you're trying to read plans while performing a particularly tricky task, are trying to keep track of what you've already accomplished and what you have yet to do, or need to write notes to yourself. Some instructions come with numbered steps with check boxes to tick off when you've completed each procedure– a handy feature. (If you haven't read it already, turn to the Gazebo project on pages 96–107. The instructions for a building should be as complete, detailed, and readable as these.)

A lumber package

You should get everything mentioned on page 135, plus the lumber required to construct the building. Be sure to get a list of any additional materials required.

A pre-cut lumber package

You should receive everything mentioned above, plus lumber that is cut to length and ready to use. Again, be sure to get a list of any additional materials required. Also, ask if any additional cutting, milling, or drilling is necessary, and make note of any tools you'll need in order to complete these operations.

A panelized package

Ask for a complete materials list before you buy. Learn what components of the building come assembled and which parts of the building process you'll need to perform. Determine the size and weight of the largest, heaviest components and take into account the people (and equipment, if required) available to you to transport these assemblies from the drop-off to the building site and to erect the building.

▼ This precut lumber package is strapped to a pallet for shipment. Lumber is banded together and color-coded to make assembly easier.

A ready-built structure

When buying a completed building, get detailed specifications of the building as you will receive it, along with an explanation of what tasks you as the building owner will be expected to perform. Some buildings are shipped completely assembled but not finished, meaning the owner is expected to paint or stain the building after arrival. Also, ask what type of site preparation and access is required upon delivery. A building delivered by a large, crane-equipped truck may have different access requirements than one delivered on a smaller, more maneuverable trailer towed behind a pickup truck. Some building manufacturers contract with delivery services that have specialized equipment, such as zero-turning-radius motorized dollies, that can maneuver a building through tight quarters and into confined, otherwise inaccessible areas. If you must remove trees or grade the approach to the site in order to facilitate delivery, figure those costs into your budget as well.

◀ Neatly boxed and wrapped in plastic, this panelized kit is ready to be loaded onto a truck for transport to its new owner.

SHIPPING COSTS

Shipping costs, of course, can be considerable, both for lumber and completed buildings. Before you get serious about selecting a building, get a rough estimate of shipping costs from the suppliers you're considering. You'll avoid agonizing over a choice between two similar buildings if a high shipping fee rules one of them out. However, don't automatically exclude far-flung manufacturers from your consideration if a distant company appears to offer a building uniquely well-suited to your purposes. In the long run, what you spend on shipping may be more than offset by having just the right outbuilding. Or you may choose to order plans and buy your materials (and labor, if you so choose) locally.

▲ A specially designed trailer transports the panelized components of a storage shed to its new location. The components are assembled by a three-person crew in about a half day. Because all the components are light enough to be hand-carried to the foundation, the building can be located in quarters that would prevent the delivery of a fully assembled structure.

Choosing Materials

If you're building your project from plans, your first step—after carefully reviewing the plans and the materials list—will likely be to purchase the materials that your project requires.

If you're ordering a lumber package, it's to your advantage to be familiar with the materials that go into making your structure. Here, you'll learn how to read lumber stamps to make sure you got the grade of lumber you ordered. You'll also learn how to check each piece of wood for quality and how to weed out any that are unsuitable for inclusion in your project.

Even if you're ordering a panelized kit or a preassembled structure, you'll appreciate this discussion of various wood species, treatments, types, and grades. The more you know, the easier it will be for you to evaluate the quality of the materials that go into the various buildings you're considering.

And lumber is not all you'll need. You'll also benefit from an overview of the fasteners and framing connectors that hold your building together and the masonry products that can serve as its foundation. You'll discover siding and roofing options, too, as a good knowledge of these materials also can help you choose from various options and upgrades.

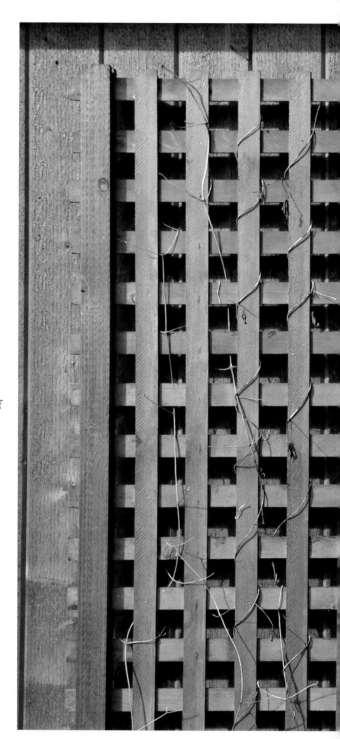

▲ Using premium materials, such as the tongue-and-groove vertical cedar siding on this shed, costs more but results in a great look, long life, and low maintenance. The iron flowerpot holders are another nice touch. Not only do they ad elegant detail, they are a low-maintenance, rot-proof alternative to wood flower boxes.

BUYING LUMBER

Wood's warm, natural beauty and remarkable workability make it ideal for backyard building projects. Select the wood for your project on the basis of its appearance, cost, and durability.

Species

Several species are commonly used for outdoor structures:

■ **Redwood, Cedar, and Cypress** Unmatched for their beauty, these softwood species are naturally resistant to weathering, warping, cupping, shrinkage, and insect damage, but they're expensive. Untreated, they weather to a silvery gray, or if you prefer, you can easily color them with stain. Cedar tends to split easily, and cypress may be hard to find. Only the heartwood is naturally resistant to decay. Use heartwood for posts and structural members fastened near or close to the ground; use sapwood treated with a sealer for rails, studs, and boards that will be visible.

■ **Fir and Pine** These species are strong, lightweight, widely available, and less expensive than naturally rot-resistant woods.

■ **Untreated Lumber** This stock is susceptible to outdoor weathering and decay if left unfinished. Not suitable for posts at all, it can be used for nonstructural members if painted.

■ **Pressure-Treated Lumber** Pine and fir that have been treated with chemicals under pressure are extremely rot resistant and less expensive than redwood, cedar, and cypress. Grade stamps tell which chemical has been used. They also tell how much preservative the lumber holds. Posts and boards that contact or are close to the ground (skids, joists, and skirts) should have a retention level of 0.60 or higher. Lumber treated to 0.40 works sufficiently for other components. Look for a "Ground Contact" or "LP22" marking.

Rot-resistant hardwoods

White oak is probably the most widely available exterior-grade domestic hardwood. It has closed cells that make it highly resistant to decay. Don't use red oak; its open-cell structure makes it

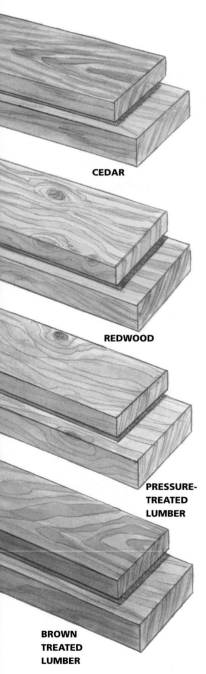

CEDAR

REDWOOD

PRESSURE-TREATED LUMBER

BROWN TREATED LUMBER

USING PRESSURE-TREATED LUMBER

Pressure treatment is not a substitute for finishing the wood. A couple of weeks after construction, apply a water-repellent sealer—several coats on surfaces you have cut.

After two or three months, apply paint or stain and after that refinish pressure-treated stock from time to time. Unfinished treated wood gradually turns to a weathered gray. Paint and other protective finishes help structures last longer.

Wear gloves when handling treated wood and a respirator when sawing it. Don't burn or bury the scrap. Check with your local environmental protection agency for proper disposal methods.

more likely to rot. The heartwood of white oak is a grayish brown, the sapwood nearly white.

Bald cypress, honey locust, black locust, and sassafras are also rot-resistant hardwoods, though all species are not available in every region.

Lumber grades

Lumber is divided into categories according to its thickness. Boards are less than 2 inches thick, and dimension lumber is 2 to 4 inches thick. Lumber is graded for its strength and appearance in accordance with standards established by independent agencies.

■ **Boards:** Fir and pine boards are graded in two categories: select and common.

Select is the best grade, with few or no knots or blemishes. Select grades are labeled A through D.

■ A contains no knots.

■ B has only small blemishes.

■ C has some minor defects.

■ D has larger blemishes that can be concealed with paint.

Common: Utility board grades are ranked from 1 to 5 in descending quality. Middle grade, such as number 3, is a good choice for most projects.

Dimension Lumber: Fir and pine dimension lumber is available in three grades:

■ Construction grade is the strongest and has the fewest defects.

■ Standard grade is almost as good as construction grade but is less expensive.

■ Utility grade is unsuitable for framing.

Pressure-treated lumber is also graded. Buy at least standard-grade dimension lumber and common-grade number 3 boards for projects.

GRADE STAMPS: WHAT THEY MEAN

Manufacturers stamp their wood products to provide customers with information about the species, prevalence of defects, grade, and moisture content. A grade stamp may also carry a number or the name of the mill that produced it and a certification symbol that shows the lumber association whose grading standards were used.

Pressure-treated lumber carries a grade stamp that shows the year it was treated, the chemical used as a preservative, exposure condition (whether it can be used above ground or have ground contact), and the amount of chemical treatment it received.

Plywood grade stamps also show whether the wood is suitable for ground contact or only for aboveground use and whether it can be used as sheathing. The stamp also specifies the thickness of the sheet and the distance it can span without support. Plywood made to withstand exposure to the weather is marked as exterior grade.

Projects can fail if the lumber used doesn't suit its application. Grade stamps help you choose lumber that meets your project's requirements.

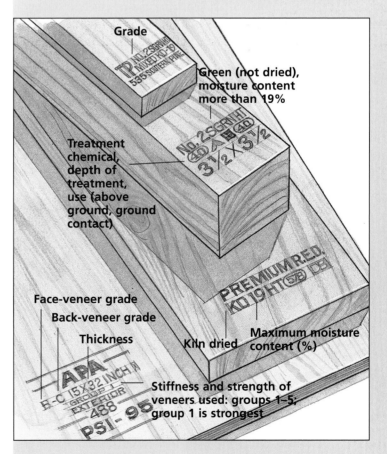

Grade

Green (not dried), moisture content more than 19%

Treatment chemical, depth of treatment, use (above ground, ground contact)

Face-veneer grade

Back-veneer grade

Thickness

Kiln dried

Maximum moisture content (%)

Stiffness and strength of veneers used: groups 1–5; group 1 is strongest

SEASONING LUMBER

Most wood is either air-dried or kiln dried. Marks specify the wood's moisture content:

- S-GRN (green lumber): more than 19 percent
- S-DRY: up to 19 percent
- MC: up to 15 percent

For framing and rough work, air-dried lumber is adequate, but S-DRY or MC 15 lumber is better. Dry stock warps less, works more easily, holds fasteners more tightly, and finishes better. Always use dry wood for finish work.

Nominal versus actual dimensions

The dimensions that describe the size of lumber, such as 1×4, 2×4, or 2×6, are nominal, not actual, dimensions. They indicate the size of the stock when it was cut from the log, before drying and milling reduced its size.

Shrinkage is generally consistent from one kind of lumber to another, although pressure-treated boards may vary slightly from untreated boards. If exact size is significant to the design you're building, measure the actual dimensions of the lumber you're using. For example, when planning a gazebo deck made of 1×6 decking, you'll want to know exactly how many boards will fit across the span of the floor, so measure the stock before fastening it.

Sheet goods

Two kinds of sheet goods are often used in outbuilding projects: plywood and oriented strand board.

- **Plywood** Manufacturers produce plywood in a variety of sizes, thicknesses, textures, species, and grades. Plywood used for outdoor construction must be an exterior-grade material made with glue that does not deteriorate when exposed to moisture. Purchase AA exterior grade for sheathing that you will stain or paint. Lesser grades work well for flooring, roof sheathing, or sheathing covered with siding, but they have blemishes that show through paint or stain. Grade stamps give you most of the information you need in buying plywood.

- **Oriented Strand Board (OSB)** OSB is a sheet material of compressed wood strands arranged in layers at right angles to each other. The strands are bonded with phenol-formaldehyde adhesive. OSB's strength and ability to hold fasteners make it an ideal—and less costly—alternative to plywood for sheathing and underlayment.

Look before buying

- **No lumber is perfect.** To get good materials for your project, walk around the lumberyard.

Take your project plans and materials list with you. Look at different species and grades to compare their colors, grain patterns, and quality. Compare pressure-treated with untreated material.

■ **Ask a salesperson to recommend project materials.** The retailer also can give you an idea of relative costs for various materials.

■ **Shop around to compare both material costs and service.** You might find a higher-grade stock costs less at one yard than lower-grade materials at another. If you can't get the material to the site yourself (for more information, see "Hauling Tools" on pages 166-167) add delivery charges to the cost of your material.

As you shop for lumber, check each board for defects. Sight down the length of the board on both the face and the edge. Look for the straightest, flattest boards you can find. Check for knots: Small or tight ones are acceptable, but avoid boards with large, loose ones. Look for checks and splits. If the wood hasn't been kiln dried, more checks and splits will develop as the lumber seasons.

Estimating, ordering, and storing

You can get a quick idea of project cost from your lumberyard visits, but ordering material requires more detail. Make a materials list that designates how much of each size stock you need, the quality of each size, and the species you want.

Be ready to tell the dealer what kind of footings you are using and how you'll finish the structure. You may be able to negotiate a better price for materials if you place the full order

▲ These boards are properly stacked and stickered to allow air circulation while drying.

with one supplier.

When the materials arrive, protect them from direct sunlight and moisture. If the lumber has not been kiln dried, let it dry for several weeks. Stack boards flat and evenly weighted, inserting spacers (called stickers) between them. Store them under a cover but don't wrap them tightly—allow for air circulation. Kiln-dried lumber is ready to use right away; protect it from moisture and direct sunlight before you begin construction.

ALTERNATIVE WOOD SOURCES

If you have an adventurous spirit, you might want to check into a couple of alternative sources of lumber. In some cases, these can provide higher-quality wood for less cost than a retail lumber outlet:

Sawmills

If you live in a wooded part of the country, you may be able to buy your lumber directly from the sawmill at significant savings. Look for them in directories under "Sawmills." Take your materials list with you but also talk to the mill personnel about the nature of your project. They may be able to suggest locally available woods that would be appropriate for your application and cost less or perform better than those your plan specifies.

▼ Got a downed tree? For a setup fee plus a set amount per linear foot sawn, many portable bandsaw mills like this one will come to you and saw your tree into lumber.

Wood purchased directly from a mill may not be grade-stamped, so you'll need to carefully inspect each piece yourself for flaws. It also may be rough-cut, rather than planed, so take into consideration how a more rustic finish will affect the look of your project. And wear gloves when handling such wood.

You may be able to choose from green or air-dried wood. If so, get the dry wood unless the green wood is available at a substantial savings. If you do buy green wood, you'll want to dry it yourself before using it (see "Estimating, Ordering, and Storing," page 143). Keep in mind that green wood is also much heavier than dry wood, due to its high moisture content, so it'll require more effort to transport, stack, and store. Green pine, spruce and fir also can bleed sticky sap that can be difficult, if not impossible, to remove from skin, clothing, and other surfaces.

A small local mill may be able to custom-cut wood to your specifications. In addition to lumber, you also may be able to purchase cedar shakes and shingles from a local mill. Some mills will deliver materials, others may require you to pick up the wood yourself. Some portable sawmills, called bandsaw mills, can be carried in the bed of a pickup truck or towed on a trailer. Many sawyers with such mills will come to you and custom-cut wood on your property to your specifications. If you have some timber that needs to be thinned—or even a single storm-felled tree—this may be the least expensive way to procure high-quality wood.

◀ If you have some room in your garage or basement, you can make a low-tech drying kiln for green lumber using a dehumidifier, a fan, a humidity gauge, and some plastic sheeting. Such a kiln will dry green wood more quickly and evenly than air-drying. A moisture meter is also useful to determine when the wood is ready for use.

Recycled lumber

Perhaps you or someone you know has a structure, such as an old garage, barn, or other building, that needs to come down. If so, you may be able to use some or all of the lumber on your new project at little or no cost. First, determine whether the lumber available is of the quality and dimensions you need. Inspect carefully for rot, water, and insect damage, as well as for flaws.

Consider the presence of existing fasteners and determine if you can easily remove them. Hitting a single metal fastener with a saw blade can ruin the saw and endanger its operator. Also consider the presence or lack of an existing finish. Weathered barn boards may be just the look you're after. However, avoid using wood that's covered with old paint, which may contain lead and can be a serious health hazard, both to work with and to have standing in your yard.

▶ Recycled lumber, such as the old barn siding that this toolshed is made out of, is often free for the asking but should be inspected carefully for damage, fasteners, and flaws before using.

FASTENERS AND HARDWARE

Just as important as the boards that go into your project is the hardware that will hold them together. Choose fasteners of galvanized or stainless steel, brass, or other rust-resistant metal.

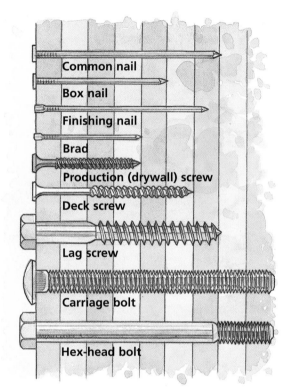

Common nail
Box nail
Finishing nail
Brad
Production (drywall) screw
Deck screw
Lag screw
Carriage bolt
Hex-head bolt

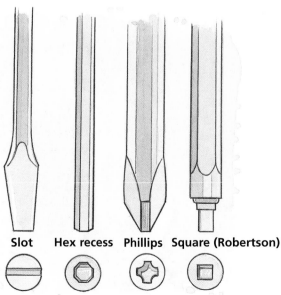

Slot   Hex recess   Phillips   Square (Robertson)

Nails

Once sold for so many pennies per hundred, nails today are sold by the pound but still described and sized by this old terminology–for example, a 16-penny or a 4-penny nail. To further complicate matters, "penny" is indicated by the letter d (for "denarius," Latin for coin). The label on the box in the hardware store identifies the size and type of nail that's inside this way: 16d common. (See the chart opposite to translate penny sizes to inches.)

Just as there are many sizes of nails, there are also many types. If you're installing plastic or metal roofing, use roofing nails with a rubber washer under the head to seal out water. You also can buy brass, copper, stainless-steel, and bronze nails. For more holding power, select spiral, threaded, or coated types. Coated nails have a transparent, resinlike covering that melts from the heat of friction as they are driven in, making them grip wood fibers better.

For small jobs, stay with 1-pound boxes of nails; some stores still sell them in bulk quantities by the pound. For most outdoor fastening jobs, you'll need common, box (same as common, but thinner), and finishing nails. Also, keep an assortment of brads on hand. Brads look like miniature finishing nails; use them for molding and finishing jobs.

Screws

Screws are rough and provide exceptional holding power in wood. They're also easy to remove, making them ideal for projects you may want to disassemble later. For projects in which fasteners will show, screws add a quality look that nails can't match.

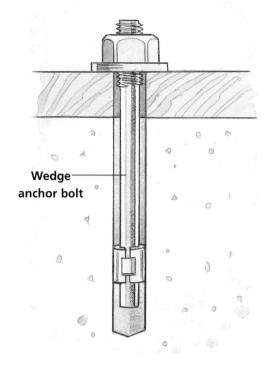

Wedge anchor bolt

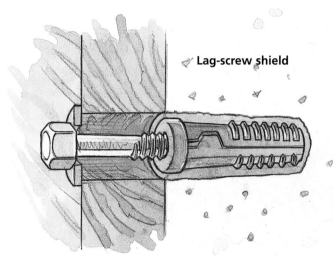

Lag-screw shield

Screw heads vary in style and slot type. Common styles are flathead, ovalhead, roundhead, and panhead. Common head types are slot, phillips, hex recess, and square.

To attach heavy objects to wood or masonry, use lag screws. These heavy-duty fasteners are good for projects with heavy framing members. Drive them into masonry using lead expansion shields like the one shown above.

Use washers with screws to prevent the screw head from pulling into or marring the material being fastened. Some washers are decorative.

Bolts

When you need a fastener that can't pull loose yet allows you to disassemble and reassemble a joint, you're literally down to nuts and bolts. If you need to fasten two items together securely and have access to both sides of the material, a two-sided fastener such as a bolt is ideal.

Bolts are sized by length and diameter. They're also classified by the number of threads per inch. For example, a ½×13×3-inch bolt is ½-inch in diameter, has 13 threads per inch, and is 3 inches long.

SIZING NAILS AND SCREWS

What size nail or screw will you need for the job? A fastener that's too small won't hold; using one that's too big risks splitting the material or poking through the material to which you are fastening.

■ Use this table to convert nail pennies (d) into inches:

3d = 1¼"	4d = 1½"	6d = 2"
7d = 2¼"	8d = 2½"	10d = 3"
12d = 3¼"	16d = 3½"	20d = 4"

■ Select nails three times as long as the thickness of the material you are fastening. For instance, to attach a 1×4 (¾ inch thick), a 6d nail (2 inches long) will be a bit short. An 8d nail (2½ inches), a little more than three times the thickness of the 1×4, will do better. If a nail is so long it will go through the base material, use a shorter nail.

■ Screws are sized by their length and gauge (diameter). The length of the screw in inches should be shorter than the thickness of the materials into which it will be driven. The smooth shank of a screw should go through the top material being fastened.

■ The gauge of screws you will need for a given project depends on the fastening strength required. Designated by number, gauges range from No. 0, which has a diameter of ¹⁄₁₆ inch, to No. 20, which is nearly ½ inch in diameter.

FRAMING CONNECTORS

Framing connectors—16- or 18-gauge galvanized metal brackets sized to accommodate standard dimension lumber—simplify the joining of major structural members in sheds and gazebos. The connectors have pre-drilled holes through which you can drive common nails (usually 12d) or, for extra strength at critical junctures, wood screws. Some connectors come with nails or include metal prongs that you drive into the wood.

Framing connectors can be bought singly, in small packages, and in bulk—25 to 50 pieces per carton. Buying in bulk can cost half as much per unit as buying singly or in small packages. The illustrations on these pages show some of the many types you'll find. The connectors available from your local dealer may not look exactly like the ones shown, but they make the same connections.

POST BEAM CAP

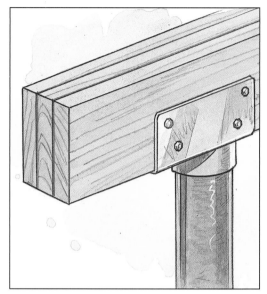

▲ Post beam caps mount on top of posts and include a channel that holds beams of varying dimensions. Manufacturers offer versions for both round and square posts in a variety of sizes, usually 4×4 or 6×6.

JOIST HANGER

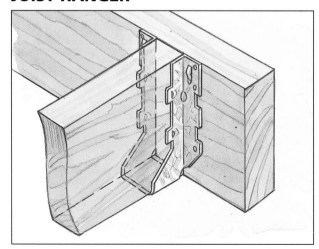

▲ Joist hangers attach joists to beams or headers in floor framing platforms and can reinforce almost any right-angle connection. Of course, you usually can attach a joist by simply nailing through the beam or header into the end of the joist or toenailing through the joist into the other framing member.

MULTIPURPOSE JOIST HANGER

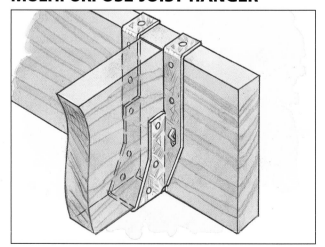

▲ Multipurpose joist hangers further strengthen joist connections with angled straps that can be nailed to the tops of boards. Again, you can save money by simply nailing or toenailing the joist in place.

ANGLE BRACKET

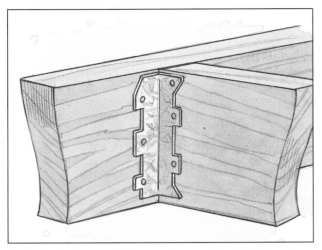

▲ Angle brackets, which come in a variety of different styles for different applications, offer yet another way to reinforce perpendicular joints. Some angle brackets attach with screws. As with joist hangers, nailing or toenailing works just as well.

▶ Hurricane ties attach notched rafters to top plates. These expensive ties are basically designed for framing that will withstand a lot of stress, such as where hurricanes, tornadoes, and earthquakes occur, and where building codes require them.

DO YOU REALLY NEED FRAMING CONNECTORS?

Unless you live where severe weather occurs, you probably can do without framing connectors for small outbuildings. Conventional joinery techniques work just as well. But connectors can speed a project along by making strong joints quickly, so they may be worth the cost—especially if their utilitarian appearance isn't noticeable or objectionable.

RAFTER HURRICANE TIES

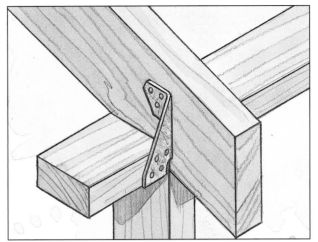

FINISHES

Here's how to select a finish that's right for your shed or gazebo: Redwood, cedar, or pressure-treated wood left unfinished will soon take on the weathered look, complete with natural checks and slight surface imperfections. The wood will eventually turn gray—a color that signals the first stage in wood deterioration. If you prefer the rich, natural hue of brand-new lumber, apply a product that forms a film on the surface of the wood. The film must stand up to harsh outdoor conditions.

Clear finishes for natural colors

Spar varnish, polyurethane varnish, water repellents, and penetrating oils shield wood from water while allowing all the color to show through. But clear finishes let ultraviolet (UV) rays penetrate into the grain. The wood cells react with those rays and begin to deteriorate under the film. The wood darkens, and the finish cracks, blisters, and peels.

Adding a UV filtering agent to the finish retards this reaction but doesn't completely eliminate it. If you use a clear finish, select one that has UV absorbers (the label will tell you). Even with UV protection, you'll have to reapply the finish at least every two years. If you wait until it peels, you'll face a tedious stripping job.

Semitransparent stains

With light pigmentation, semitransparent stains let the wood's natural grain and texture show through. These stains are available in tones that closely match various woods. Brighter stains can either contrast with or complement your house, deck, or patio. Semitransparent stains usually have an oil base and only fair resistance to UV, so you'll have to reapply the finish every year or two.

Semisolid stains have more pigment than semitransparent stains and offer more UV resistance as well. But they're not completely opaque. You can expect a semisolid stain to last about two years.

Opaque stains

Like paint, opaque stains conceal the wood's natural color. Unlike paint, they allow the

Water repellent   **Solid-color stain**   **Semisolid stain**   **Paint**

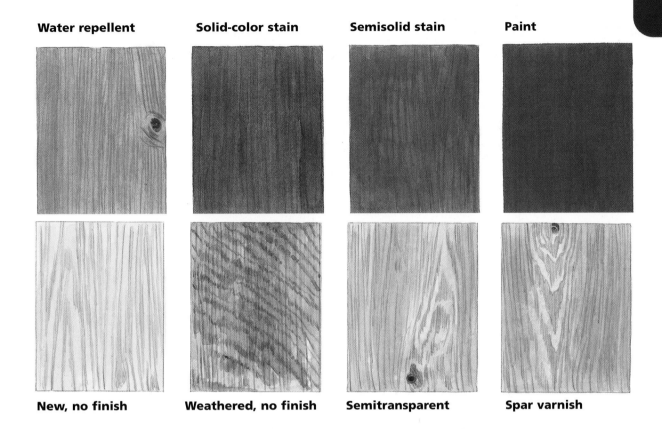

New, no finish   **Weathered, no finish**   **Semitransparent**   **Spar varnish**

texture to show. They're available in a variety of natural-looking colors and brighter hues and with either an oil or latex base. You also can choose either a flat opaque stain or a low-luster finish that's easier to wash.

Because the pigment in this type of stain is suspended in an oil or latex carrier, it's possible that it won't penetrate all wood surfaces equally. Especially on horizontal surfaces, pigment that doesn't completely penetrate may collect, causing blotchy areas that wear off or blister. The California Redwood Association doesn't recommend using stains with a latex base on redwood products. Opaque stains usually need to be recoated every two years.

Select a compatible stain color for treated lumber because the chemical used to treat the wood imparts a color of its own that tends to alter the final appearance. Experiment with several different stain colors on treated wood

(use scraps left over from the project) until you achieve the effect you want. (Some stain manufacturers offer special 4-ounce samples that you can experiment with before you select a particular product.) If you buy a building in kit or lumber package form, check with the package manufacturer about finishes. They often can recommend some that work particularly well with their materials.

Paint

Paint is rarely used on the top grades of redwood or cedar because it hides grain, texture, and color—prime attributes of such woods. But paint can be your solution to hiding the hue of treated lumber, and is often recommended for best protection of sheet goods such as T-111 siding. It's also the only way to protect unplated steel parts from rust.

TOOLS

Tools are the means to the end: The right ones will help you do the job quickly, safely, and well. Carefully chosen, high-quality tools are a good investment—not only for your current project but for future ones as well. As your familiarity with what they can do increases, you'll find more uses for them. Good tools pay for themselves again and again—not only in money saved by not having to hire professionals to assemble your building for you but in the freedom and pride that comes from knowing that you have the means to alter and improve your property to suit your needs and lifestyle.

As you assemble a collection of tools for outbuilding work, start by purchasing only those tools you need for the job at hand, then gradually add to your collection as the scope of your work expands. That can be more easily said than done, because tool buying is *fun*. So many good tools are out there—and they can help you do so much—that it can be easy to justify overbuying. You probably don't need the top-of-the-line, most expensive models. But buying good-quality tools from the start means your purchases will last through many years of service.

This section will walk you through the different kinds of power and hand tools that you might need for outbuilding construction. You'll learn about safety equipment, tool accessories, and some popular, multifunction tools that pack many functions into units that are easy to use and store. You'll read about rental tools, and find some suggestions as to how to organize, transport, and store your tools so what you need will always be handy. Finally, you'll discover hauling tools that will help you get your materials and equipment to your building site.

▶ **Good-quality tools make your job easier and more pleasurable, and in the case of fine hand tools, they may well serve your needs for a lifetime. Fortunately, most of the tools you need for erecting an outbuilding can be put to use on just about any other construction project you can imagine.**

LANDSCAPE TOOLS

The landscaping tools you'll need for backyard building projects vary with each specific project, but you should have at least some of these implements on hand.

Drain spades have a narrow rounded blade that's ideal for digging trenches. They're also handy for shoveling dirt or concrete around posts that you're setting.

Hand augers screw into the ground to bore holes for posts.

Clamshell posthole diggers do the same job in a different way, by grabbing and lifting out a chunk of earth at a time.

Drain spade

Hand auger

Clamshell posthole digger

Iron rake

Round-blade shovel

Tamper

Trowel

Iron rakes, also called bow rakes and garden rakes, break up and level soil.

Round-blade shovels are all-around digging tools. A square-blade spade (not shown) is best for digging up sod and slicing through small tree roots.

Tampers compact soil around posts and in other spots that require firm, dense earth.

Trowels move small amounts of soil in tight spots. They also are useful for mixing concrete and placing it around posts.

ELECTRONIC LEVELS

Classic bubble levels are precision instruments, but they have a few limitations. Because even mason's levels measure four feet or less in length, drawing a longer plumb or vertical line—on a building, for example—requires sliding the level. And every time you move it, you risk inaccuracy that will compound as you progress. Electronic levels such the laser models shown above project a light beam that makes a plumb or level line on a surface that's as long or high as the surface itself. A buzzer sounds to indicate level or plumb.

RENTAL TOOLS

A couple of specific tools can make an outbuilding job go a lot faster, but they are expensive to buy and bulky to store, especially if you're only going to use them occasionally. Fortunately, you can rent these tools by the day at a reasonable cost from a local rental center.

■ **Power Posthole Diggers** come with interchangeable spiral boring bits for making holes 6, 8, 10 or 12 inches in diameter. They can excavate holes up to 44 inches deep. The larger auger takes two people to operate and is less likely to kick out of a hole when it hits a rock or tree root. Although the other auger can be operated by one person, you'll probably need two people to heft the tool.

■ **Electric Concrete Mixers** feature large barrels that typically hold about 2 cubic feet of wet concrete. They take the hard work out of preparing the mix. Again, you'll need a helper to move the mixer in and out of your delivery vehicle.

Hand Tools

Measurement and layout tools

These tools will help you throughout a project as you plan, lay out, and build.

1. Tape measures provide a compact ruler for all measuring tasks. Thirteen-foot models are most common and slip easily into a pocket; 26-footers are bulkier but will handle just about any measurement you'll need to perform.

2. Combination squares allow you to draw square lines across boards for cross cutting. Such a square is also handy for marking layouts a specific distance in from the edge of a board.

3. Layout squares (also called speed squares) do many of the same tasks as a combination square. They also serve as circular saw guides, allowing you to make perfectly square crosscuts. Some models allow you to make cuts at various angles, which makes

cutting roof rafters, for example, easy.

4. Framing squares can be used for larger layouts.

5. T-bevels transfer angles from one place to another.

6. Levels come in many lengths. Start with a small, convenient-to-carry torpedo level. You'll also want a 3- or 4-foot carpenter's level for doing accurate, large-scale work.

7. Plumb bobs are simply heavy, pointed weights. When dangled from a string, a plumb bob and the string will provide a plumb vertical reference.

8. Chalk lines are used to draw long, straight lines. Get one that reels into a weighted metal

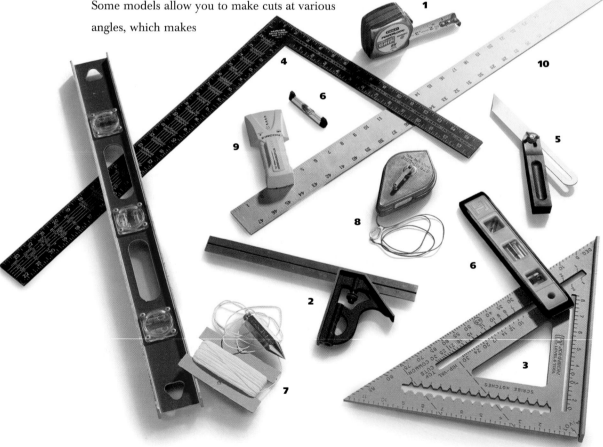

case that serves as a plumb bob and can be filled with powdered chalk. The string is rechalked every time you rewind it.

9. Stud finders help you "see" through walls.

10. Metal straightedge rules are handy for marking straight lines.

Construction Tools

When you're ready to start building, these tools are the essentials.

1. 16-ounce claw hammers are heavy enough to drive large nails yet small enough for use when installing moldings.

2. 21-ounce framing hammers will let you drive large quantities of big nails faster.

3. 12-ounce tack hammers provide the control you need for installing trim.

4. Nail sets drive finishing nails below the surface of moldings.

5. Screwdrivers in a variety of tip types and multiple sizes are necessary for driving

fasteners and installing hardware.

6. Awls mark hole locations and start screws.

7. Utility knives do everything from sharpening your pencil to cutting roofing shingles and material packaging.

8. Coping saws are great for cutting moldings at inside corners.

9. Miter boxes and backsaws make accurate crosscuts and miters in molding; a motorized version is called a power miter box.

10. Chisels pare wood to fine-tune the fit of door hinges and other hardware. Purchase a set with ¼-inch, ½-inch, ¾-inch, and 1-inch blades.

11. Planes make short work of smoothing, straightening, and squaring wood.

12. Heavy-duty metal snips come in handy for a variety of cutting tasks.

13. Bar clamps hold materials in secure alignment while fastening them.

14. Spring clamps hold smaller objects in alignment, or act as a third hand when needed.

PAINTING TOOLS

Painting tools are perhaps the least complicated and most familiar tools of all. Quality is a concern for paintbrushes and rollers. Don't skimp or you'll be disappointed in the results.

1. Roller trays and liners hold paint for rollers. Disposable liners make cleanup a snap.

2. Trim rollers paint small surfaces.

3. Drop cloths and masking tape protect any surface you don't want painted.

4. Rollers and handles apply paint to wide swaths of surface area.

5. Paint guards move along with your brush to keep paint off adjoining surfaces.

6. Brush combs straighten paintbrush bristles and aid in cleaning brushes.

7. Paintbrushes and angled sash brushes are used for trim, cutting in, and window sashes.

8. Edgers create neat, sharp lines where two surfaces meet.

9. Roller handle extension poles allow you to paint tall walls or ceilings without a ladder. They're also handy for painting floors.

POWER SAWS

our types of power saws will accomplish almost everything you'll need to do when building a shed or gazebo.

1. A 7¼-inch circular saw crosscuts and rips lumber and plywood to the right size, making straight cuts with ease. If you buy only one power saw, this is the one to get. Steel blades dull quickly, so purchase the more durable carbide-tipped combination blade.

2. A saber saw crosscuts and rips, though much more slowly and with less smoothness and accuracy than a circular saw. A saber saw's main function is cutting curves, but it is also indispensable for making small cutouts of any shape, as its thin blade can start a cut almost anywhere that you can drill a small starter hole. Some models feature variable speed control, which is handy if you cut materials other than wood, such as plastic or metal. An orbital-cutting saber saw cuts faster than one without this feature.

3. A reciprocating saw features a variety of blades with teeth designed to cut different materials—including wood, nails, screws, and even steel pipe. Its blade can reach into tight places, such as between framing members.

4. A power mitersaw is a stationary circular saw and is also called a chop saw. It makes quick, clean crosscuts, but its real forte is making extremely accurate miter (angled) cuts. If you have a lot of trim pieces to cut and install, a chop saw is the tool to use.

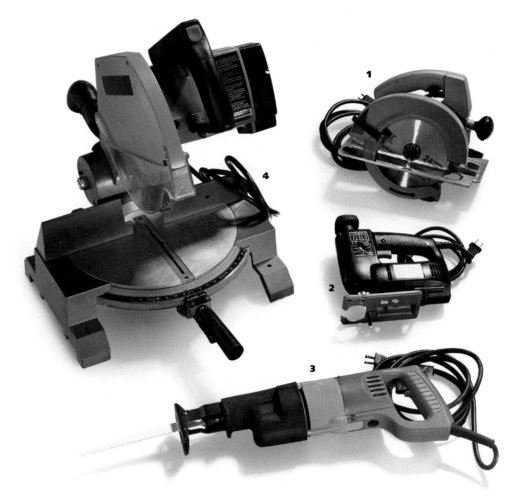

DRILLING AND SHAPING TOOLS

A drill and some bits are all you need for most work. Add a router and you can make your own moldings.

1. A ⅜-inch variable-speed, reversible (VSR) drill can handle almost all drilling needs. If you're going to be drilling lots of holes in concrete, consider getting a hammer drill, which can be set to add an impact action similar to a jackhammer to help speed drilling in masonry. Otherwise, a good, upper-mid-grade corded drill will do fine. Low-cost, homeowner-grade models and cordless models lack the power or the heavy-duty guts necessary to handle repeatedly holes with hole saws and large spade bits.

2. Twist drill bits bore such things as pilot holes for screws. Buy a graduated set of these.

3. Router bits shape wood into moldings. Buy only the profiles you need for your project.

4. Hole saws are powered by a drill to make really large holes.

5. Routers cut decorative moldings.

6. Belt sanders aggressively smooth and shape wood.

7. Random-orbit sanders produce a smooth finish suitable for sanding, painting, or staining.

CORDLESS POWER TOOLS

Cordless tools have revolutionized the market. The most popular is the cordless drill-driver, but you'll also find cordless reciprocating saws, circular saws, jigsaws—even miter saws.

Cordless tools bring increased portability and convenience to a project. While especially useful if you're working far from an electrical outlet, these tools have some disadvantages:

■ They usually cost more than corded versions.

■ Use and run time depend on the battery charge and capacity. The tool must be kept charged to be ready for use. (If you buy one, keep two batteries. Use one while the other is recharging.)

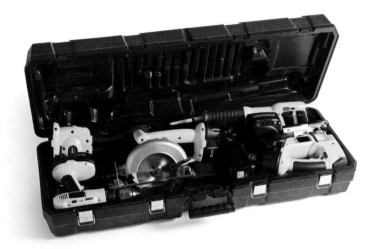

■ Worn-out batteries are expensive to replace.

■ Cordless-tool batteries range from 7.2 to 24 volts. Drills come in a range of voltages; other tools have higher-voltage battery packs.

■ Some cordless tools simply aren't powerful enough for some jobs, such as drilling into concrete or making repeated bores with big bits.

■ Cordless drills, for example, are often heavier and larger than their corded counterparts, making them somewhat more fatiguing to hold and difficult to use in tight spots.

Cordless tools are generally sold with a charger designed to recharge that tool's battery. You'll find nickel-cadmium (nicad) batteries in most tools you shop for, but those with nickel metal hydride (NiMH) batteries are generally worth the extra cost. They provide more run time and faster recharging with less weight. If you own more than one drill-driver, the second should definitely be cordless, ideally 12 volts or more, with a ⅜-inch chuck, a two-speed transmission, and an adjustable clutch that kicks the motor out of gear when it reaches a preset torque level. The last feature keeps you from breaking or burying screws as you drive them.

BUY QUALITY

Many of today's medium-priced tools boast features, power, and durability that once could be found only in pricey professional-grade tools. A homeowner-grade tool, however, might be a smart buy if you will use it infrequently for jobs in which continued accuracy isn't a requirement. The best rule to follow for tool purchases is this: Buy only the tools that you really need—but buy the highest-quality tool you can afford.

When comparing tools, use amperage ratings to compare power, rather than horsepower ratings, which can be deceiving. In general, tools that are more durable and long lasting feature ball or needle bearings instead of bushings, precisely machined gears instead of die-cast or nonmetallic gears, one-piece housings, switches with dust boots, and hatches that allow you to change worn-out brushes.

SAFETY EQUIPMENT

Buy these pieces of safety equipment at the same time you buy the tools that require their use.

1. Industrial-quality safety glasses or goggles–the ones with side shields–protect your eyes. Look for a "Z87.1" label on the glasses or goggles; that tells you they're industrial strength. If you wear prescription glasses, either buy prescription safety glasses or get goggles that fit over your glasses. Try goggles on before you buy them. Find a pair so comfortable that you won't mind wearing them all the time while working.

2. Earplugs or muffs offer hearing protection from noisy power tools. Try them on before you buy to find the most comfortable pair. If they are not comfortable, you will be less likely to wear them.

3. Dust masks protect your lungs during dusty operations such as sawing, sanding, and drilling holes in concrete. Check the label before you buy and match the mask to the type of work you will be doing.

4. Work gloves help you handle dirty work such as unloading materials and cleaning up debris. Do not wear them when you are working with power tools–you are more likely to lose your grip or fumble a tool or piece with gloves on. Gloves can also get caught in a spinning blade or drill bit. Rubber gloves keep your skin from becoming dry and irritated when applying paint.

5. Boots are a good footwear choice when you are using power tools; their cowhide skin offers more protection against cuts and bruises than does lighter footgear. At the very least, wear sturdy, rubber-soled shoes to prevent slipping when you're working.

ACCESSORIES

Several items make working with hand and power tools easier.

1. Extension cords Purchase heavy-duty ones–the wires should be 12 gauge. Lightweight cords can overheat, posing a fire or shock hazard, and they will rob the tools of the power they need. Always use three-pronged cords and grounded receptacles. When working outdoors, plug the cord into a ground fault circuit interrupter (GFCI). Uncoil the cord so it doesn't develop kinks, which can damage the conductors. Protect the cord from sharp edges and, if it crosses a walkway, tape it down with duct tape.

2. Sawhorses hold lumber at a comfortable working height. You can create an impromptu worktable by nailing a sheet of plywood between two horses. Wooden horses are heavier than metal models, but they do have some advantages. You can nail a couple of 2x4s across them for added stability. Also, you won't damage your saw blade if you happen to cut into a wooden sawhorse.

3. Work lights make it simpler and safer to work in dimly lit spaces. Halogen models throw a brighter, whiter light than incandescent lights and often come with adjustable stands. Be careful, though–they get very hot.

3

2

1

MULTIFUNCTION TOOLS

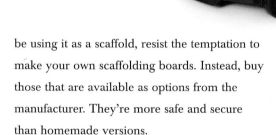

Some multifunction tools are a poor compromise, an attempt to do too much with too little. Others, however, are so versatile and well-designed you'll wonder how you ever got along without them. Here are a few favorites, in the order of increasing size:

1. Portable workbenches, sometimes called clamping benches, can be plunked down anywhere you need a work surface. The top is split in two, and a pair of cranks moves the two top pieces back and forth to hold material you're working on. Pegs slip into holes in the tabletop, allowing you to grab even wide or irregularly shaped pieces. The table can also be used to hold tools—such as a miter box—firmly while in use. They fold flat for storage.

2. Combination ladders perform the function of a whole collection of ladders, and then some. They consist of four 4-foot-long ladder sections that are jointed together to fold up like an accordion into a neat, rectangular package that's easy to transport. On the work site, you can use it as a 4-, 8-, 12-, or 16-foot straight ladder (depending on how many sections you unfold), a 4- or 8-foot double stepladder, or an 8-foot-long, 4-foot-high work scaffold. You can also use it in an L shape as a roof scaffold. Get one with joint latches that are easy to use and click positively in place and a commercial-duty, 300-pound rating. Even if you weigh half that or less, you'll appreciate the rigidity of a high-capacity ladder. And if you'll

be using it as a scaffold, resist the temptation to make your own scaffolding boards. Instead, buy those that are available as options from the manufacturer. They're more safe and secure than homemade versions.

3. Shop vacuums are an essential antidote to the inevitable messes building projects create. Choose the combination wet-dry type; you'll be glad to have the ability to quickly suck up standing water and spills. Some vacuums have a detachable power head that allows you to convert it to a portable blower—great for cleaning large areas. For serious work, get the 2-inch-diameter suction hoses; the smaller, 1¼-inch hoses tend to clog frequently. Smaller hoses work great, though, when you're using the device as a portable dust-collection system; these hoses will connect to the sawdust discharge ports on many tools. You don't need a huge machine—easy portability is often more important than huge capacity.

TOTING TOOLS

1. Tool pouches are perhaps the best time- and frustration-saving tools you can buy. Without one, you'll be constantly interrupting your work as you fetch tools you forgot to have on hand. Get in the habit of wearing your pouch and storing tools in the same pockets all the time. When you do, you'll find that you reach for the right tool without thinking about it, freeing your mind to concentrate on the job at hand and thus, adding to your safety.

2. Tool bags are a great way to organize and transport the tools

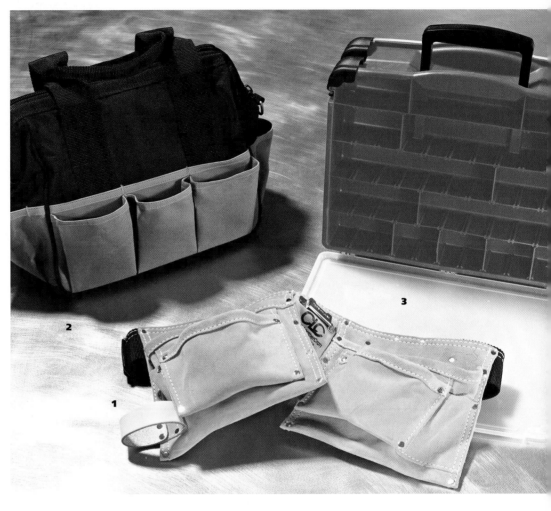

you use most frequently. These look like old-fashioned doctor's bags, with loop handles and wide-opening gate mouths, except they're made of heavy canvas or cordura nylon instead of black leather. A multitude of pockets inside and out keeps tools organized and handy, and a huge main compartment is big enough to hold a power tool or two as well as the usual assortment of hammers, chisels, pry bars, and wrenches. Like soft-sided luggage, these bags expand with the load. They also don't rust, clank around, or mar floors as metal boxes can.

3. Plastic organizer cases store and

transport fasteners and hardware. Get one with movable dividers so you can accommodate different-size items. These portable cases are about the size of a small attaché case, with sturdy carrying handles. One type is divided down the middle, and each side is covered with a snap-down, clear plastic lid. In one side, you can carry an assortment of nails, brads, tacks, and staples; in the other, a variety of screws. For big jobs such as framing or roofing, of course, you'll need to buy fasteners by the pound. But for most small jobs, this kit will have what you need—and make it easy to find.

HAULING TOOLS

Constructing an outbuilding—or even just preparing a site and foundation for a completed building—can involve transporting quite a bit of heavy stuff: bulky, heavy rental tools, lumber, concrete mix, gravel, landscaping materials such as mulch or landscaping blocks or timbers, even good-sized plants and small trees. And projects of this nature can be addictive—once you've experienced the satisfaction of making one major property improvement, you may well find other projects you'd like to undertake. So—how are you going to get all those materials home? If you already own a truck, you may be set. If not, you have several options:

■ **Pay for delivery.** For a fee, almost anything can be delivered, and sometimes that's the way to go, especially for something, such as a large

▲ This trailer has a ¾-ton cargo capacity, and a bed that can be configured as a 4½x8 foot box for hauling bulk landscaping materials or a 4½x12-foot flatbed for toting lumber. The front and rear gates are removable, and the rear gate can be configured as a loading ramp. The axle can be positioned in two different locations for optimum weight distribution, and the tongue extends and tilts to further facilitate loading and towing. The cost: about $700, brand-new. Add an extra $100–200 for a trailer hitch and electrical wiring, and another $100 or so for a transmission cooler.

tree, that requires specialized equipment to haul and/or install. However, scheduling a delivery for exactly the right time is sometimes difficult. Also, it means you have to order bulk materials, such as lumber, gravel, or topsoil, in one large lot. This can mean living with a mountain of gravel blocking your driveway or killing your lawn—and you still have to transport it in cartloads to the exact spot where and when you need it.

◄ This old pickup serves all the hauling needs of four families. Each contributed $225 toward the $900 purchase price when they bought the 16-year-old vehicle, and each buys their own gas and kicks in $100-$200 a year or so for insurance, maintenance, and registration. A trailer hitch adds to the vehicle's versatility and carrying capacity.

■ **Rent a truck.** If you're in a position to get all of your materials at once, it may be cheaper for you to rent a truck for a day than to pay delivery fees to several different retailers. In addition to rental outfits, many car dealers rent trucks and vans, and most major home center chains offer you the use of a pickup or similar vehicle for a small fee to take one or more large items home. This also can be more convenient than ordering a delivery, as you can time your rental to meet your schedule. But it's still not as convenient as toting materials home with your own equipment.

■ **Buy a set of roof racks.** If you're working on a small project and the only bulky stuff you'll be buying is lumber and sheet goods, you may be able to get away with a set of roof racks. Check first to make sure your car is robust enough to accept them. Roof racks have the advantage of distributing weight over all four wheels of your car—a safer option than overloading the trunk. Loading and unloading involves heavy lifting, a strong partner, and care to avoid damaging your car in the process. An added benefit: Such racks are useful for transporting ladders and other bulky items, too, and some systems allow you to use them as ski racks, bike racks, and cartop carriers, adding to their versatility.

■ **Buy tie-downs.** If you're transporting tools, lumber, or other large, bulky, heavy, or awkward items, secure them well, or your load could end up littering the highway—or coming loose and injuring you during transport. Bungee cords don't have the strength required for most tie-down purposes, and ropes can easily work loose. For the most secure load, use ratcheting nylon straps. These lever-action devices are smaller versions of those used to secure multiton loads to flatbed trucks. Their flat, nylon strap has tremendous tensile strength, and the ratcheting device allows you to snug your load so tight it'll feel as though its bound with steel bands. The straps are available in a variety of capacities—get heavier ones than you think you'll need and look for good-quality ratchets that are plated for rust resistance and coated with rubber to protect your vehicle's finish. Inspect the straps after each use for signs of abrasion and replace any that look questionable.

NOW THAT YOU HAVE IT HOME...

You'll need something to move everything from tools to gravel around your property. Again, you have choices:

■ **Contractor's Wheelbarrows** are the traditional option. The large, inflatable tire on the front floats over the soft soil often found around construction sites, but they have their disadvantages: They tip over easily, and the load isn't centered over the wheel, straining your back.

■ **Garden Carts** such as the one pictured above are often a better option, particularly if you don't have to deal with carrying heavy loads through deep mud. They have large, bicycle-style wheels that roll easily over obstacles and uneven ground. Weight is centered over the axle, so you don't have to lift the load—just push and guide it. And two wheels make such carts stable, both while rolling and when parked.

RESOURCES

Sheds and gazebos are available in plan, lumber package, panelized kit, and completed building form from a variety of suppliers throughout North America. Those that follow are a good place to start. For more sources, both local and national, search directories under "Sheds," "Gazebos," "Barns," and "Outbuildings."

Plans:

Better Barns

126 Main St. S, Bethlehem, CT 06751

888/266-1960; www.betterbarns.com

Gardensheds Web

651 Millcross Rd., Lancaster, PA 17601

717/397-5430; www.gardensheds.com

Jamaica Cottage Shop

P. O. Box 106, Jamaica, VT 05343

866/297-3760; JamaicaCottageShop.com

Better Homes and Gardens®

Reader Shopping Service, Dept. 0004, Box 9128, Des Moines, IA 50306-9128

800/881-4066. Specify Best Little Garden Shed.

Kits:

Gardener's Supply Company

128 Intervale Rd., Burlington, VT 05401

800/688-5510; www.gardeners.com

Jamaica Cottage Shop

P. O. Box 106, Jamaica, VT 05343

866/297-3760; JamaicaCottageShop.com

Spirit Elements

1495B Yarmouth Ave., Boulder, CO 80304

800/511-1440; www.SpiritElements.com

Summerwood, Inc.

733 Progress Ave., Toronto, Ontario M1h 2W7, Canada. 800/663-5042; www.summerwood.com

Assembled Buildings:

Better Barns

126 Main St. S, Bethlehem, CT 06751

888/266-1960; www.betterbarns.com

Odds and Ends

Dennis Verhey

1142 Hwy. 102, Pella, IA 50219

Gardensheds Web

651 Millcross Rd., Lancaster, PA 17601

717/397-5430; www.gardensheds.com

Jamaica Cottage Shop

P. O. Box 106, Jamaica, VT 05343

866/297-3760; JamaicaCottageShop.com

Walpole Woodworkers

767 East St., Walpole, MA 02308

508/668-2800; www.walpolewoodworkers.com

Vixen Hill Pavilions

P.O. Box 389, Elverson, PA 19520

800/423-2766; www.vixenhill.com

BUYING GUIDE

Interested in learning more about a shed or gazebo you've seen pictured in this book? The following guide is a page-by-page, photo-by-photo listing of the source of each building pictured. Contact information for all sources mentioned in this buying guide are listed in "Resources," beginning on page 168. No further information is available about buildings referred to as "custom" in the list below.

4. Custom.

5. Left: Custom. Center: Better Barns. Right: Custom.

6.-9. Jamaica Cottage Shop.

10. Bottom Right: Jamaica Cottage Shop.

11. Top right: Summerwood, Inc. Middle Right: Better Barns. Bottom: Better Barns.

12. All: Custom.

13. All: Odds and Ends.

14. Custom.

15. Custom.

18-19.. Gardensheds Web.

20.-23. Better Barns.

24. Top: Spirit Elements, Inc. Bottom: Jamaica Cottage Shop.

25. Top: Better Barns. Bottom: Spirit Elements, Inc.

26. All: Spirit Elements.

27. Top: Better Barns. Bottom: Jamaica Cottage Shop.

28.-31. Garden Sheds Web.

32-33. Custom.

34.-36. All: Better Barns.

37: All: Custom

38. All: Jamaica Cottage Shop.

39. All: Spirit Elements.

42-43: Walpole Woodworkers.

44.-47. All: Better Barns.

48.-51. Jamaica Cottage Shop.

52. Top left: Spirit Elements. Middle right: Better Barns. Bottom Left: Custom.

53. Top right: Better Barns. Bottom left: Custom. Bottom right: Spirit Elements.

54. Custom.

55. Vixen Hill Pavilions.

56. Custom.

57. All: Custom

58. Custom.

59. All: Custom.

60. Custom.

61. Top: Vixen Hill Pavilions.

62-63. All: Custom.

64. All: Vixen Hill Pavilions.

65. All: Custom.

66. All: Custom.

67. All: Custom.

71. Top left, top right: Vixen Hill Pavilions. Bottom: Better Barns.

72. Jamaica Cottage Shop.

74. Jamaica Cottage Shop

82-83. Summerwood, Inc.

110.-111. Gardener's Supply Co.

113. Better Barns.

116. Better Barns.

121. Jamaica Cottage Shop.

117. Left: Jamaica Cottage Shop. Center: Gardener's Supply Co.

120-121. Jamaica Cottage Shop.

122. Custom.

123. Vixen Hill Pavilions

124. Jamaica Cottage Shop.

125. Vixen Hill Pavilions

126.-127. Better Barns.

128.-129. Better Homes and Gardens®)

131. Top: Custom. Bottom: Walpole Woodworkers.

132.-133. Gardener's Supply Co.

134. Better Barns

136. Jamaica Cottage Shop.

137. Top: Summerwood. Bottom: Better Barns.

138.-139. Better Barns.

145. Bottom: Odds and Ends

GLOSSARY

A-B

Actual Dimension. True size of a piece of lumber.

Batten. A narrow strip of wood used to cover joints between boards or panels.

Batterboard. A board frame supported by stakes set back from the corners of a structure.

Beam. A horizontal support member.

Bearing wall. An interior or exterior wall that helps support the roof or the floor joists above.

Bevel cut. A cut through the thickness of a piece of wood at an angle other than 90 degrees.

Blind-nail. To nail so that the head of the nail is not visible on the surface of the wood.

Board. Any piece of lumber that is less than 2 inches thick and more than 3 inches wide.

Board foot. The standard unit of measurement for wood. One board foot is equal to a piece 12×12×1 inches (nominal size).

Butt joint. The joint formed by two pieces of material when fastened end to end, end to face, or end to edge.

C-F

Cantilever. A beam or beams projecting beyond a support member.

Casing. Trim around a door, window, or other opening.

Chalk line. A reel of string coated with colored chalk, used to mark straight lines.

Chamfer. A bevel cut made along the length of a board edge.

Concrete nails. Hardened steel nails that can be driven into concrete.

Control joint. A groove tooled into a concrete slab during finishing.

Cripple. A short stud above or below a door or window opening.

Darby. A long-bladed wood float commonly used to smooth the surface of freshly poured concrete.

Dimension lumber. A piece of lumber that is at least 2 inches thick and at least 2 inches wide.

Drywall. A basic interior building material consisting of sheets of pressed gypsum faced with heavy paper on both sides.

Eaves. The lower edge of a roof that projects beyond the wall.

Edger. A concrete finishing tool for rounding and smoothing edges.

Fascia. Horizontal trim attached to the outside ends of rafters or to the top of an exterior wall.

Float. A rectangular hand tool used to smooth and compress wet concrete.

Footing. A thick concrete support for walls and other heavy structures built on firm soil and extending below the frost line.

Framing. The skeletal or structural support of a building. Sometimes called framework.

Frost line. The maximum depth frost normally penetrates the soil during the winter.

G-L

Gable. The triangular area on the end of a building's external wall located beneath the sloping parts of a roof and above the line that runs between the roof's eaves.

Galvanized. Coated with a zinc outer covering to protect against oxidation.

Grain. The direction of fibers in a piece of wood; also refers to the pattern of the fibers.

Hardwood. Lumber derived from deciduous trees, such as oaks, maples, and walnuts.

Header. The framing component spanning a door or window opening in a wall and supporting the weight above it.

Hip. The outside angle of a roof formed by the intersection of two sloped sides of the roof.

Jack studs. Studs on both sides of a door, window, or other opening that help support the header. Sometimes called trimmers.

Jamb. The top and side frames of a door or window opening.

Jointer. A tool used for making control joints, or grooves, in concrete surfaces.

Joist. Horizontal framing member that supports a floor or ceiling.

King studs. Studs on both ends of a header that help support the header, and run from the wall's soleplate to its top plate.

Lag screw. A screw with a hexagonal head.

Lap joint. The joint formed when one member overlaps another.

Load-bearing wall. A wall that supports a wall or roof section on the floor above.

M-R

Miter joint. The joint formed when two members that have been cut at the same angle meet.

Molding. A strip of wood used to cover exposed edges or as decoration.

Mortar. A mixture of masonry cement, masonry sand, and water.

Mortise. A shallow cutout in a piece of wood usually used to recess hardware such as door hinges and latches.

On center (OC). The distance from the center of one regularly spaced framing member or hole to the center of the next.

Particleboard. Panels made from compressed wood chips and glue.

Partition wall. A wall that supports no structure.

Plumb. The condition that exists when a surface is at true vertical.

Rafters. Parallel framing members that support a roof.

Rake. The inclined edge of the roof of a building.

Ready-mix. Concrete that is mixed in a truck as it is being delivered.

Rebar. Steel rod used to reinforce concrete and masonry.

Reinforcing wire mesh. A steel screening used to reinforce concrete.

Retaining wall. A wall constructed to hold soil in place.

Ridgepole. Topmost beam at a roof's peak.

Rip. To saw lumber or sheet goods parallel to the grain.

Rise. The vertical distance from one point to another above it; a measurement you need in planning a stairway or ramp.

Riser. The upright between two stairsteps.

S-Z

Sash. The part of a window that can be opened, consisting of a frame and glass.

Screed. A straightedge, often a 2×4 or 2×6, used to level concrete as it is poured into a form and to level the sand base in a form. Also, the process of leveling concrete or a sand base.

Set. The process during which mortar or concrete hardens.

Setback. The distance a structure must be built from property lines (dictated by local zoning ordinances).

Setting nails. Driving the heads of nails slightly below the surface of the wood.

Shake. A shingle that has been split, rather than cut, from wood.

Sheathing. The first covering on a roof or exterior wall, usually fastened directly to the rafters or studs.

Shim. A thin piece of wood or other material used to fill a gap between two adjoining components or to help establish level or plumb.

Siding. Planks, boards, shingles, or sheet goods used as an external covering of the walls of a building.

Sill. The lowest horizontal piece of a window, door, or wall framework.

Slate. A rough-surfaced tile that has been split, rather than sliced, from quarry stone.

Slump. The wetness of a concrete or mortar mix; the wetter the mix, the more it spreads out, or slumps.

Soffit. Covering attached to the underside of eaves.

Softwood. Lumber derived from coniferous trees, such as pines, firs, cedars, or redwoods.

Soleplate. The bottommost horizontal part of a stud-framed partition. When a plate rests on a foundation, it's called a sill plate.

Spalling. Cracking or flaking that develops on a concrete surface.

Span. A distance between supports.

Square. The condition that exists when two surfaces are at 90 degrees to each other. Also, a tool used to determine square.

Straightedge. An improvised tool, often a 1×4 or 2×4 with a straight edge, used to mark a line on material or to determine if a surface is even.

Stringer. The main structural member of a stairway.

Studs. Vertical 2×4 or 2×6 framing members spaced at regular intervals within a wall.

Stud finder. Electronic or magnetic tool that locates studs within a finished wall.

Subfloor. Usually plywood or another sheet material covering the floor joists.

Template. A pattern to follow when re-creating a precise shape.

Timber. A structural or framing member that is 5 inches or larger in the smallest dimension.

Toenail. To drive a nail at an angle to hold together two pieces of material.

Top plate. The topmost horizontal element of a stud-frame wall.

Valley. An intersection of roof slopes.

Warp. Any of several lumber defects caused by uneven shrinkage of wood cells.

Yard. The unit of volume by which ready-mix concrete is sold; equal to 27 cubic feet.

INDEX

A-C

Access, 22
Acrylic sheets, 106–107
Angle bracket, 149
Arbor, 30
Asphalt shingles, 57, 111
Base map, 118–119
Block foundation, 112–113
Board-and-batten siding, 16, 49
Bolts, 147
Boxed-in base, 41
Brass hardware, 71
Brick path, 53
Bubble plan, 122
Cedar boards, 17, 22
Cedar shakes, 10, 14, 39
Cedar shingles, 10, 12, 16, 47,
    105–107
Cement pad foundation, 86
Cold frame, 30
Concrete foundation
    block, 40, 112–113
    poured, 84–85
Cordless power tools, 161
Cupolas, 11

D-F

Decking, gazebo, 103
Deck-top gazebo, 62–63
Details, 68–71
Dormer, 95, 97
Drainage, 127
Drills, 160
Easements, 119
Entertainment, space for, 67
False stone foundation, 40, 48
Fasteners, 68, 146–147

Faux slate, 10, 34
Finials, 15, 37
Finishes, 150–151
Flagstone path, 53, 64
Floors, 33, 78, 87–88, 112
Focal point, 38, 56, 60–61, 65, 120
Foundations
    cement pad, 86
    concrete, poured, 84–85
    concrete block, 112–113
    garden shed, 84–86
    gazebo, 100
    materials, 40–41
    post, 100
    potting shed, 112
    skid, 48, 77, 113
    on slopes, 41, 113
    woodshed, 77
Framing
    garden shed, 87–95
    gazebo, 101–104
    woodshed, 78, 79
Framing connectors, 148–149

G-K

Garden sheds
    building project, 82–97
    design ideas, 28–39
Gazebo
    building project, 98–109
    deck-top, 62–63
    design ideas, 38, 55–67
    garden, 64
    landscaping, 61
    lighting, 66–67
    location, 60
    on slopes, 58–59

Golf-course gazebo, 62
Grade, lumber, 141
Grading, 127
Grass path, 52
Gravel
    floor, 112
    pad, 6–7, 23, 41, 77
    path, 53
Greenhouse, 32–33, 110, 120, 121
Guest shed, 43
Hand tools, 156–157
Hardware, 69–70, 146–147
Hinges, 69, 70
Hobby shed, 44–45
Hurricane ties, 149
Instructions, 135–136
Joist hanger, 148
Kits, 39, 82–83, 97, 110, 138, 168

L-O

Ladders, 164
Landscape tools, 154–155
Landscaping, 25, 61, 119
Lap siding, 17, 39
Latches, 69, 70
Lattice, 14–15, 59
Layout tools, 156–157
Levels, electronic, 155
Lighting, 58, 66–67
Lightning rods, 11
Location
    gazebo, 60
    north edge of lot, 120
    orienting on a slope, 27
    restrictions, 118–119
    site analysis, 120–123
    storage shed, 24–27

sun and wind considerations, 121

woodshed, 8

Lumber

dimensions, 142

grades, 141

package, 136, 138

pressure-treated, 140

recycled, 145

from sawmills, 144

seasoning, 142–144

shopping for, 142–143

wood species, 140–141

Master plan, 122

Materials

choosing, 138–151

fasteners and hardware, 146–147

finishes, 150–151

foundation, 40–41

framing connectors, 148–149

lumber, 140–145

path, 52–53

roof, 10

shipping costs, 137

siding, 16–17

Measurement tools, 156–157

Metal roof, 10, 50, 81

Nails, 68, 146, 147

Office shed, 42–43

Outdoor rooms, 122

Outhouse-style sheds, 12–13

P-S

Paint, 151

Painting tools, 158

Panelized buildings, 110–115, 136, 137, 138

Path lighting, 58

Paths, 52–53

Pea gravel, 14, 33, 41

Permanent versus nonpermanent buildings, 119

Pier blocks, 113

Planning

base map, 118–119

choosing a product type, 135–137

site analysis, 120–123

site preparation, 126–127

size of structure, 124–125

style choice, 130–131

Plans. See also Projects

bubble, 122

choosing, 132–133

customizing, 22

instructions, 135–136

landscape-design software, 123

master, 122

rendering, 133

sources of, 168

study, 132

Pool shed, 46–47

Porch, 27, 34, 38

Post beam cap, 148

Post foundations, 100

Potting sheds

building project, 110–115

design ideas, 28–39

Pressure-treated lumber, 140

Projects, 73–115

garden shed, 82–97

gazebo, 98–109

potting shed, 110–115

woodshed, 74–81

Railing, gazebo, 107–108

Ramps, 22–23, 27, 53

Random-width siding, 16, 49

Recycled lumber, 145

Rendering, 133

Rental tools, 155

Restrictions, 118–119

Retreat sheds, 48–49

Ridge cap, 15, 81

Roof

adornment, 11

construction, 79, 81, 104–107, 114

gable roof assembly, 92–95

glazed, 110

materials, 10

Rough-sawn board siding, 16, 74–75

Rustic sheds, 22–23, 48–49

Safety equipment, 162

Sawmill, buying lumber from, 75, 144

Saws, power, 159

Screen room, 50–51

Screws, 146–147

Setback requirements, 119

Shaping tools, 160

Shelving, 45

Shipping costs, 137

Siding

applying, 80, 89–93

materials, 16–17

Site analysis, 120–123

Site preparation, 126–127

Size, 124–125

Skid foundation, 48, 77, 113

Skylights, 30, 65, 98, 106

Slate, faux, 10, 34

Slope

foundations on, 41, 113

gazebo on, 58–59

orienting shed on, 27

INDEX (CONTINUED)

Soffit, 96, 105

Software, landscape-design, 123

Special-purpose sheds, 42–51

    hobby, 44–45

    lakeside, 42–43

    pool, 46–47

    retreat, 48–49

    screen room, 50–51

Stains, 150–151

Stairs, 109

Stepping stones, 52, 57, 61

Stone facing, 40, 41

Storage sheds

    design ideas, 18–27

    location, 24–27

Story poles, 26, 124

Studio shed, 42

Study plan, 132

Style, 130–131

Sun, shed location and, 121

T-Z

Textured 111 (T-111) siding, 17, 36

Tin can siding, 16

Tongue-and-groove siding, 17, 35, 39, 45, 89, 138

Tools, 152–167

    accessories, 163

    buying quality, 161

    construction, 157

    cordless power, 161

    drilling and shaping, 160

    hand, 156–157

    hauling, 166–167

    landscape, 154–155

    measurement and layout, 156–157

    multifunction, 164

    painting, 158

    power saws, 159

    rental, 155

    safety equipment, 162

    toting, 165

Toolsheds, 12–15

Trellises, 36

Trim, 80, 96–97

Utility lines, 119

Vacuums, shop, 164

Vegetation, removing, 126

Walls, 89–91, 114

Weather vanes, 11

Wheelbarrows, 167

Wind, shed location and, 121

Windows, 32–33, 71

Woodsheds

    building project, 74–81

    design ideas, 6–9

Workbenches, 164

Zoning regulations, 118–119